MW01256891

Slow Burn

Slow Burn

The Work and Wonder of the Wait

DAWNCHERÉ WILKERSON

W PUBLISHING GROUP

AN IMPRINT OF THOMAS NELSON

Slow Burn

Copyright © 2025 DawnCheré Wilkerson

All rights reserved. No portion of this book may be reproduced, stored in a retrieval system, or transmitted in any form or by any means—electronic, mechanical, photocopy, recording, scanning, or other—except for brief quotations in critical reviews or articles, without the prior written permission of the publisher.

Published in Nashville, Tennessee, by W Publishing, an imprint of Thomas Nelson.

Thomas Nelson titles may be purchased in bulk for educational, business, fundraising, or sales promotional use. For information, please email SpecialMarkets@ThomasNelson.com.

Unless otherwise noted, Scripture quotations are taken from the ESV® Bible (The Holy Bible, English Standard Version®). Copyright © 2001 by Crossway, a publishing ministry of Good News Publishers. Used by permission. All rights reserved.

Scripture quotations marked GW are taken from *God's Word*®. Copyright © 1995 God's Word to the Nations. Used by permission of Baker Publishing Group. All rights reserved.

Scripture quotations marked THE MESSAGE are taken from *THE MESSAGE*. Copyright © 1993, 2002, 2018 by Eugene H. Peterson. Used by permission of NavPress. All rights reserved. Represented by Tyndale House Publishers, Inc.

Scripture quotations marked NIV are taken from The Holy Bible, New International Version®, NIV®. Copyright © 1973, 1978, 1984, 2011 by Biblica, Inc.® Used by permission of Zondervan. All rights reserved worldwide. www.Zondervan.com. The "NIV" and "New International Version" are trademarks registered in the United States Patent and Trademark Office by Biblica, Inc.®

Scripture quotations marked NKJV are taken from the New King James Version®. Copyright © 1982 by Thomas Nelson. Used by permission. All rights reserved.

Scripture quotations marked NLT are taken from the Holy Bible, New Living Translation. © 1996, 2004, 2015 by Tyndale House Foundation. Used by permission of Tyndale House Publishers, Inc., Carol Stream, Illinois 60188. All rights reserved.

Scripture quotations marked TPT are taken from The Passion Translation®. Copyright © 2017 by BroadStreet Publishing® Group, LLC. Used by permission. All rights reserved.

Any Scripture in italics is the author's added emphasis.

Any internet addresses, phone numbers, or company or product information printed in this book are offered as a resource and are not intended in any way to be or to imply an endorsement by Thomas Nelson, nor does Thomas Nelson vouch for the existence, content, or services of these sites, phone numbers, companies, or products beyond the life of this book.

Cover design: Faceout Studios, Spencer Fuller
Original Package Design: © 2025 Thomas Nelson
Cover art: © Shutterstock
Author photo: © Yesi Laver
Interior design: Kait Lamphere

ISBN 978-1-4003-4553-3 (audiobook)
ISBN 978-1-4003-4552-6 (ePub)
ISBN 978-1-4003-4551-9 (TP)

Library of Congress Control Number: 2024952621

Printed in the United States of America

25 26 27 28 29 LBC 5 4 3 2 1

JANUARY 24, 2013

GOD,

Your faithfulness on this journey has swept me off my feet.

The pain never stayed.

Your grace has inhabited my heart. Before I hear a heart-beat and before I hold them close, I want you to know you will always be my heart. You will always be my source. I can go without others but you I can't go a day without.

You are my promise.

My reward.

My peace and completion.

My joy and friend.

So real to me is your presence. I can't go a day without you.

I want what YOU want. With ALL my heart. That is my request.

I want my life to glorify the name of JESUS.[a]

---

a. See appendix for the handwritten journal entry.

This book is dedicated to:
Wyatt, Wilde, Waylon, and Wolfgang.

Before your life began.
Before it was your time.
You were already mine.[b]

b. See appendix for the handwritten journal entry.

Contents

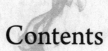

CHAPTER 1

Will You Live in the Wait?

The table is set and the candles will soon be lit.

Any moment now, my extended family members will burst through the door to welcoming embraces and unspeakable joy after their long flights to Miami. My husband, Rich, just got home with a chocolate cake from the bakery down the street. My best friend from college is in the kitchen, arranging sunflowers in table vases with care. Music fills the house as my kids, Wyatt, Wilde, and Waylon (ranging from ages three to six), race around the dinner table with their scooters like it's the Indy 500.

I've found a quiet place in the front seat of my minivan after returning home from errands, and it feels like the perfect cocoon for reflection before the festivities begin.

I'm turning forty.

I still feel like a kid in many ways, yet I know I'm a long way from the little Cajun girl from a big Louisiana family of six kids. With my dad as both a football coach and a fiery preacher, I spent every weekend watching the pigskin game under Friday night lights and singing hymns on Sunday morning. I'm also far from the seventeen-year-old who recorded pop music in Nashville, dreaming big dreams, and who fell in love with a preacher's son. Now, I sit in my driveway in Miami, decades away from those

1

days, in a completely different life and a place I've called home for seventeen years.

On this birthday I have been married to Rich for eighteen years; we have three kids and one on the way. We walked through eight years of infertility, ultimately moving from a desert of barrenness to a life of miraculous fruitfulness—which began far before we had our first child. We have gone from youth pastors to church planters. For almost a decade we have led a gritty, loving church in the heart of Miami.

I've now had four decades of getting to know more and more of the Father's heart and living out his story for me. Like everyone's story, mine has involved years of waiting—waiting for courage and a strong sense of identity, for a calling and marriage, for children and church growth, and the list goes on.

I am sure you have your own list too.

I think of how God used long stretches of time to accomplish what he wanted in and through people in Scripture—and how the number *forty* specifically played a significant role in many of their stories.

The Israelites wandered in the desert for forty years before they entered the promised land. Noah and his family endured forty days on the ark, surrounded by what I'm sure felt like endless waters. Goliath taunted the Israelites for forty days before David courageously confronted him. Jesus fasted and prayed in the desert for forty days before he was tested by the Enemy and then stepped into a new season of power. The disciples shifted from soul-crushing sorrow to awe-filled joy during the forty days between the crucifixion and the ascension.

While the period of forty days or years has a literal meaning, it also can symbolize testing and trials. Moses spent forty years in Egypt and then forty years in the wilderness before God ignited his biggest calling at the burning bush. He'd then embark on yet another forty-year period! After all those years, it was only the beginning of a new season for Moses.

Sometimes we are in a place like Moses was, thinking perhaps the key points in our story are behind us, when we're actually in the middle, in between turning-point moments. Moses was in a waiting place, not at the end.

Other times we know full well we're in a waiting place—and it is stretching out, feeling relentlessly long. It seems like we just finished waiting on something else not long ago! Inclined to resent the wait, we can assume it is a boring, random part of our lives to trudge through.

I operated with this perspective—though I may not have admitted it or even been able to articulate it—until God got a hold of my heart with a game changer.

The wait is not just a season.

The wait is life.

And then the question became, *Will you live while you wait?*

Maybe today you are in the middle, in between the "major" moments of your life. What are you waiting on? Do you question whether it is too late for God to do it?

And do you wonder if there is something worthwhile that can happen until then—even now?

His Best Work on Our Souls

Humans do not instinctively wait well. We tend to buck against it, even hate it. Entire industries have been created just to shorten our waits. Distractions are welcome if they'll somehow bring our desired outcome more quickly; many of us just scroll until the time miraculously passes. We assume there is no value in waiting, and, over time, we feel the wait wearing us down.

Years ago I hit a point when I decided the blessings I longed for would never come. Today I'm living in a season defined by those blessings. I sit squeezed into the front seat of my minivan, my stomach expanding each day with the life within me. It's taken me forty years to reach this season of carrying our miracle baby boy—and I can see now it did not come a moment too soon.

God had more forming work to do in me.

And God's forming work takes time. *A lot* of time.

Ronald Rolheiser offered a fascinating picture of this in his book *The Holy Longing*. Discussing how human faces develop distinctive features, he explained how French philosopher Jean-Paul Sartre believed that the beauty of a newborn's face relies primarily on genes. "But, with each hour, day, and year of its life, this changes and . . . culminates at age forty when, finally, a person has the essential lines of a face." At that point a face displays "individuality, character, and a beauty-beyond-genes."

How we choose to live day after day, year after year, makes us who we are, and it's written all over our faces.

Rolheiser concluded,

What is important about all of this is what, in the end, forms our faces. Up until age forty, genetic endowment is dominant, and that is why, up until that age, we can be selfish and still look beautiful. From then onward, though, we look like what we believe in. If I am anxious, selfish, petty, bitter, narrow, and self-centered, my face will show it. Conversely, if I am warm, gracious, humble, and other-centered, my face will also show it. A scary thought; there can be no poker faces after forty.[1]

Development never comes overnight. It takes a lifetime.

If I'd had my first child at the time of my choosing, I wouldn't have half the perspective I hold now. What I gained in the wait has made all the difference in my ability to steward this season and has given me strength to be patient in the way I need to be now.

God wasn't punishing me; he was preparing me.

And so it is in every sphere of my life.

Over the years I often have felt behind, like life had given me a deadline I couldn't ever meet. Unexpected delays, goals pushed back, and then last-minute sprints to the finish line. Fashionably late is still a thing, right? I sure hope so.

Even now, I had planned to turn this manuscript in months ago. But if I had, I would not have been able to share this moment in the minivan, where I'm surveying the big picture of my journey thus far, amazed at what only God could have orchestrated.

He finishes what he starts with unique and supernatural precision if we will wait on him. And so I'm not "behind"; I'm existing in his timeline. He is faithfully leading and creating the story he wants to tell. I am in the middle of it, and his presence right here makes me smile.

What is the wait worth? I'm reminded of an old rumored story about Pablo Picasso, when a woman approached him at a café.

> [She] asked him to scribble something on a napkin, and said she would be happy to pay whatever he felt it was worth. Picasso complied and then said, "That will be $10,000."
>
> "But you did that in thirty seconds," the astonished woman replied.
>
> "No," Picasso said. "It has taken me forty years to do that."[2]

While I am no Picasso, I believe every life creates priceless art from the human experience. It took me forty years to write this book. This book is my life. And what is the cost of having something worth writing about? Forty years of testing, waiting, and holding on to a promise that will truly be fulfilled only in eternity, when I'll be face-to-face with my Creator and have no pain, no tears, and endless peace.

No more waiting is what I'm still waiting on.

I'm decades into my story, and yet it's not the end; it's the middle. The "in-between."

The same can be said of you, no matter what age you are. If you know Jesus, you are on the same journey I am, heading for the true forever home, not there yet but well on our way. This book is for anyone who has struggled in the wait or might say the "in-between" feels like a stuck place.

But the amazing news is, you aren't stuck; you're living in a miracle. Right here, right now.

Again, waiting is not part of life. Waiting is life. The issue of your earthly journey is not, *When will I no longer have to wait?* It's, *Who am I becoming in the wait?*

It is not about the cards you have been dealt. It's about the cards you surrender.

When you surrender to God day after day in the wait, you experience inner transformation—the kind that prepares you for what comes next. In fact, I believe that "what comes next" can't be fully realized or experienced unless we are deeply reshaped first.

This played out in David's life. Samuel anointed him as the next king when David was only a boy; it took many years for it to become a reality. Throughout the wait God formed David through many slow-burn circumstances, from leading a group of outcasts to become victorious in battle to living on the run as King Saul obsessively hunted him. David developed a deep faith that he brought into the large calling of ruling Israel. The wait humbled him, strengthened his discernment, tested his heart, and trained him to rely fully on God.

amazon.com®

SBqXfcjvL1

Order of May 21, 2025

Qty.	Item
1	**DJWJFJEN Mustard Seed NeckIace Jewelry Baptism Confirmation Gifts for Teen Birthday Graduation Religious Catholic Faith ...** X004575NKJ CD–Seed Mountain–S02 **(Sold by DaJinDianZi)**
1	**Slow Burn: The Work and Wonder of the Wait** Wilkerson, DawnChere --- Paperback **1400345510** 1400345510 9781400345519

Return or replace your item
Visit Amazon.com/returns

0/BqXfcjvL1/-2 of 2-//HOU5-NIT/second-nominated-day/0/0521-14:00/0521-07:55

B3-10

A gift for you

Enjoy your gift! From Samantha Teal

amazon Gift Receipt

Scan the QR code to learn more about your gift or start a return.

Slow Burn: The Work and Wonder of the Wait

Order ID: 112-9369431-2355441   Ordered on May 21, 2025

David couldn't have known all that God was doing in him at the time. Only years later could he look back and see the effects of daily communion with God.

As a man after God's heart, David repeatedly wrote throughout the Psalms, "I will wait on you, Lord." He waited on God

- for deliverance
- for direction
- for forgiveness
- for refreshing
- for healing
- for vindication
- for confidence

If we want to be people after God's heart, we must be people who wait. He created us to wait on him in every season to find our direction, comfort, strength, healing, revelation, joy, and hope. Our daily waiting is where we will find our daily destiny—and where God reshapes us.

As Charles Swindoll once put it, "We don't like waiting, but that's when God does some of His best work on our souls."[3]

Our Best Offering to Him

The candles on my table will burn slowly throughout the entirety of my birthday dinner this evening, illuminating the night, then reach their end with a last breath of smoke.

We often think our lives will culminate to a mighty bonfire or dynamite explosion, but that explosion is eternity that awaits. Here on earth our lives are a constant, steady slow burn of faith through the wait.

Of course, we typically live more like we are following the words of a talent agent: "It's not about what you're doing now; it's about what's next." The goalposts keep moving, so when we reach a finish line, we find we are waiting again. At that point, the state of our heart can be summed up in the joke, "I had my patience tested, and I'm negative."

If we are meant to embrace the wait, *what do we do* while we wait—especially when it seems we are just burning time?

Consider the wisdom we can glean from the ancient practice of burning incense.

The word *incense* comes from the Latin word *incendere*, which simply means "to burn."[4] God instructed Moses to have Aaron burn incense on the tabernacle altar, placing the incense near a heat source so it could smolder over an extended amount of time. Moses and Aaron set their incense on coals, and when they did, it released an aroma that filled the tabernacle.

God wanted them to do this every single morning and night. This twice-a-day offering the priests presented on behalf of the Israelites was an act of worship. A perfumer provided the ingredients of the incense, and the rising smoke represented the people's prayers to God. The fragrant sacrifice was to be "salted and pure and sacred," just like our very lives (Exodus 30:35 NIV).

Every human life is like a vapor, here today and gone tomorrow. God invites us to make our lives an act of worship, relying on him as our heat source to produce rising smoke. We are to surrender to him morning and night and for all the extended time in between.

As we do, the smoldering effect leaves a scent for our Father, one that delights his heart and draws the lost to him with the "aroma of Christ" (2 Corinthians 2:15). It's also a fragrance that reminds us of our surrender to him as our source.

Humans are excellent at distinguishing different scents.

Recent studies have shown we're capable of identifying a trillion different aromas![5] What we smell can influence our thoughts and be linked with past moments. The scent of honeysuckle sends me to my backyard in Louisiana, Cajun spice reminds me of high school crawfish boils, and a perfume I used in the first year of dating Rich takes me back to our sweet early moments together. Smell and emotion are stored as one memory, tied deeply together.

God told the Israelites to use a specific sacred blend of incense for worship. He wanted his people to associate a scent with their fragrant offerings because they *needed a reminder* to remain in worship or return to it. He knew that, in the daily wait of life, they would forget their source and their purpose. They'd trade out the slow burn, which pointed to all that is sacred, for a flash in the pan, which was easy but empty.

God knows that you and I operate the same way today.

How quickly we forget him in the wait! How often we bring our best offering each morning and night to everyone *but* God. We spend our lives on meaningless dreams and dead-end pursuits.

We rush ahead instead of waiting on God.

Tom Petty said it best: "The waiting is the hardest part. Every day you get one more yard. You take it on faith, you take it to the heart. The waiting is the hardest part."[6]

But perhaps the hardest is the holiest.

The Constant, Steady, Slow Burn of Faith

"If the Lord Jehovah makes us wait, let us do so with our whole hearts; for blessed are all they that wait for Him," wrote Charles Spurgeon. "He is worth waiting for. The waiting itself is beneficial to us: it tries faith, exercises patience, trains submission, and endears the blessing when it comes."[7]

Wholehearted waiting. What a thought. Research has shown that driving while distracted on your phone slows down your journey and inhibits the flow of traffic.[8] So it is when we wait half-heartedly. We are distracted by the future we long for and dissatisfied with our present reality, so our pace becomes stagnant and our flow is stifled.

Wholehearted pursuits yield the greatest harvests.

There were seasons when God's people didn't just wait half-heartedly; they forgot all he had done and offered their incense to false gods. They "went after worthlessness, and became worthless" (Jeremiah 2:5).

The same struggle of the heart remains in our culture today. We are too busy waiting on everything but God. And he is the only one worth waiting on.

God once told his wandering people how they would later give him honor: "In every place incense and pure offerings will be brought to me, because my name will be great among the nations" (Malachi 1:11 NIV).

When Jesus walked the earth, he "gave himself up for us, a fragrant offering and sacrifice to God" (Ephesians 5:2). He became a fragrant offering so our lives could become an offering too—so we could do what Paul described in Romans 12:1: "In view of God's mercy, to offer your bodies as a living sacrifice, holy and pleasing to God—this is your true and proper worship" (NIV).

And we know the praise will continue in heaven. We read in Revelation, "The smoke of the incense, mixed with the prayers of God's holy people, ascended up to God from the altar" (8:4 NLT).

He is forever worthy of all we can bring him.

So again: What do we do while we wait, when it seems we are just burning time?

We live like David, who told God, "Every morning I lay out

the pieces of my life on the altar and wait for your fire to fall upon my heart," and, "Let my prayer be counted as incense before you, and the lifting up of my hands as the evening sacrifice!" (Psalm 5:3 TPT; 141:2).

Making our lives a fragrant offering means trusting God wholeheartedly in the slow burn. We choose to steward our thoughts, motivations, conversations, and worship in the wait.

Will there be moments when that feels impossible? Of course. We are *human*; our emotions and limited perspectives can lead us to simply cope however we can and forget coming to God altogether. But he knows this. He understands our struggle. He will meet us where we are and help us.

When God spoke to Moses at the burning bush, he showed his heart for his people. "I have indeed seen the misery of my people in Egypt. I have heard them crying out because of their slave drivers, and I am concerned about their suffering. So I have come down to rescue them from the hand of the Egyptians and to bring them up out of that land into a good and spacious land, a land flowing with milk and honey" (Exodus 3:7–8 NIV).

Look at his extraordinary love in action: "I have *seen* your misery, I have *heard* your cries, I'm *concerned* about your suffering, and I have *come* to rescue you."

He's saying the same to his children today.

I first truly encountered the love of God as a teenager when he gave me the strength to step through my fear. The freedom I experienced was unlike anything I had ever known. I'll tell you all about it later in our journey together. And how, throughout the years since, he has proven himself faithful time and time again, meeting me in my struggle, pouring out love, and empowering me for every next step.

I know he'll do the same for you, too, as you open up more of your life to him in the wait.

A Lifetime of Discovering His Heart

My table for tonight is set with special names embroidered on each napkin, the treasured people who will fill the seats. The permanence of the gesture hints at their permanent place in my life, including the love of my life, the best friend from college in Tennessee, and the family from Louisiana. They have walked with me through the wildernesses of waiting and celebrated on the mountaintops of my journey, again and again, as is the cycle of life.

One special seat at the table tonight has a napkin with the name of a person I haven't met yet. "Wolf" it reads in goldenrod thread, my fourth child, who is already loved and welcomed as we wait for his arrival. I'm waiting throughout this forty-week journey to see this boy's face, and once I do, I'll patiently wait as the purpose of God continues to faithfully unravel in all our lives moment by moment, year by year. I will keep my hands open to him and discover who he wants us to become throughout the wait.

It is not a single moment of trust but a lifetime.

Friends have jokingly reminded me that I'm "over the hill" this week, the symbolic midway mark of the journey and life expectancy. To me, the journey to year forty has felt much more like climbing a mountain than gliding over a hill. Either way, as I look back at God's loving-kindness to me, I'm choosing to pitch a tent right here and make an altar. I want to stay in awe of the God who has brought me this far. I will make these pages a memorial stone to my faithful Father and Friend.

Would you like to join me in your own way as we step forward together? Maybe you'll grab a journal to write out how God meets you in the wait or find a friend to process what he's stirring in you both throughout each chapter ahead.

May all who pass by hear our testimony of his goodness in the wait.

The fire of our lives will one day be extinguished, but when the fire fades, may the fragrance remain. And may the first directive in Exodus be the story of all history—that "incense will burn regularly before the LORD for the generations to come" (30:8 NIV).

I know that until that point there are more mountains ahead for us. I for one want to keep returning to the same altar again and again to surrender the rest of the journey home. If you join me, you'll find what I have so far: There will be work, and there will be wonder.

Our work will be coming to God and trusting. The wonder will be sensing his joy.

Our work will be surrendering. The wonder will be knowing his faithfulness.

Our work will be giving him our attention. The wonder will be getting glimpses of heaven.

We're in the wait, you and me—on a pathway to discover the heart of God.

Let's go see what he'll show us next.

CHAPTER 2

Strike a Match

I was driving down a familiar road headed to a familiar office when I heard words that took my breath away.

"Uncle Ro went to be with Jesus last night. His cancer procedure didn't go as planned."

My mom's voice from the phone seemed to echo in the silence that followed. I paused at the stop sign as the Miami sun shone through my windshield, and tears streamed down my face.

Uncle Roosevelt had become family to us when he moved from Manhattan to Louisiana to work with my father when I was nine years old. He quickly became a beloved part of our close-knit "Ragin' Cajun" family—with six kids—and was known for jovially engaging in epic pillow fights. He was explosively joyful with an iconic laugh, like a staccato hiss that hit again and again in perfect time. And whenever Uncle Ro spoke at our church, he called me up to the front to sing before he shared. The bond between the two of us became so strong over the years that, even after I moved away from Louisiana, he'd call me whenever he was traveling within a few hours of Miami. "Come minister with me at this service, DawnCheré." It filled my heart every time I joined him.

He and I had been together only months before this devastating moment. I hung up with my mom. I went through the motions of driving to my doctor's office while in shock. Thinking back to the last day I'd seen Uncle Ro. Considering his wife and children's great loss.

It was my twenty-fifth birthday, and I had been married for almost four years to the love of my life, Rich. We had long been eager to create a nest of our own and felt ready for our first baby. I had notified my doctor and she had run routine blood tests.

After I was led to an examination room and waited a bit, the doctor marched into the room and, with no preamble, reported, "Your blood tests have come back, and they are irregular. You are going to have trouble having kids." Grabbing a business card out of her white coat and handing it to me, she continued, "Here's an infertility specialist. Make an appointment. They'll take it from here."

I'm usually a very guarded person, but I couldn't stop the tears that suddenly began falling again. I reached out for the card while stammering, "I'm s-sorry, I lost a loved one this morning. That's what the tears are about. I'm fine."

In a dry tone she replied, "I'm sorry for your loss," and strode out.

Feeling I was now in an alternate universe, I left the doctor's office and drove to work, to the office of the church Rich and I worked at, where his parents were lead pastors. In the elevator, I wiped away the last encore of my tears and hit the button to close the elevator door. *So this is twenty-five. Happy birthday.*

Surely the doctor had it wrong—my mother had given birth to six children with no problems. My dad winked at her and she got pregnant. *This isn't my story. I won't let it be,* I told myself. *I'll figure this out.*

Little did I know I was beginning an eight-year journey of waiting that would involve massive personal transformation. I would become a completely different person from that twenty-five-year-old by the time I held my first miracle in my arms.

Could those eight years of barrenness actually have birthed more in me than any other seemingly fruitful season?

Was that twenty-fifth birthday the embryonic start of a brand-new creation within me, ushering in a deeper strength and grace to have with me the rest of my journey?

Perhaps my twenty-five years on earth had been leading me to this very moment.

Teach Me, Lord, to Wait

The day I was born, my parents gave me a life scripture. They wanted a promise of God to mark my life and be a handle I could hold on to with faith in every season. They chose Isaiah 40:31: "They who wait for the LORD shall renew their strength; they shall mount up with wings like eagles; they shall run and not be weary; they shall walk and not faint."[c]

Music is the life source of our family; it marks our culture and family bond, so it only made sense that my uncle Teddy Grover wrote a song inspired by the life scripture my parents chose for me. I grew up singing that song again and again—in churches and nursing homes, in my parents' studio where they wrote and produced music, at family gatherings and in everyday moments. Even now it resounds in my heart like a faithful friend. The simple chorus of Uncle Teddy's song is Isaiah 40:31 verbatim, and then the last line of the chorus simply says, "Teach me, Lord, to wait."

Have you ever prayed a prayer without knowing it?

I look back on the thousands of times I sang that song over the years and can see the power of my prayer with twenty-twenty

---

c. See appendix for the handwritten journal entry.

vision. The declaration of faith I sang was a prophetic statement for my life journey.

I asked God to teach me to wait. And he did.

In a sense, my life journey is no different from yours. You know about struggling with the tension of earth and eternity, present and future, pause and press. You don't need to have Isaiah 40:31 as a life verse or a song about it from your upbringing to know about waiting. You've endured much over arduously long stretches of time. You are living it now.

Maybe for you it's the healing process of a bodily injury or relational wound.

The surgery and chemo you're persevering through and wondering if it will be effective.

The dream job that has yet to open up or the life partner you've not yet found.

It could be postdivorce stability or relief from grief you're longing for.

Or the clear leading about a big life change and what you are meant to do next.

Waiting is inescapable.

And while we might feel like a whole lot of nothing is going on in a slow burn, we couldn't be more wrong.

There most definitely is something going on.

This Is Where You Can Transform

My husband, Rich, recently started using a sauna, and he could be a sales rep the way he preaches its benefits. I, unfortunately, am not a fan. Yes, I have heard the positive effects dry heat can have on my health—lowering blood pressure and reducing the risk of stroke, cardiovascular disease, and serious heart conditions. It can decrease cortisol levels and chronic pain, it can detoxify the body, and it can improve sleep and respiratory function.[1] Even though I know *all of that*, I still just don't like waiting in the stinking heat.

But I will not deny how powerful the effects of heat are—or how this reality deepens the imagery of a slow burn.

The heat of life transforms us. Like bread in the oven or pottery in the kiln, like fruit becoming preserves or logs of wood becoming embers—we are changed moment by moment into what seemed impossible before we encountered the heat.

The heat of life expands us. Thermal expansion is the increased molecular movement that occurs in substances when they're heated. The pressure in car tires rises along with the temperature because heat makes the air in them expand. You can't see the change happening at the molecular level, but the change is indeed happening.

Think of how incense alone can't fill a room with a scent; it's just a tiny lump of granular spice. But when you place it on a heat source, its scent can reach every corner of a space.

The same thing happens with the little offering you put on the altar. When it rests on the heat God supplies, it supernaturally expands beyond your own ability and creates lasting, powerful impact. Day and night, the little you hold as you wait is transformed as you choose to lay it on the altar.

The heat of God reshapes, refines, and empowers us.

The heat of the world causes pain and comes at us from all different directions.

But what I know about God is that whether we're dealing with divorce, heartbreak, sickness, loneliness, betrayal, or confusion, he will use our pain to serve his purpose. We always can keep trusting him to do that.

When we don't trust him, though, our pain can lead us to waste the wait. To wander through it. Or to worry through it.

People often live however they want to in a season of single-ness, glorifying selfish pursuits and individual endeavors, then think they can jump into marriage with ease. They'll suddenly become the new person they'll need to be for the new season.

Cue the wrong-answer sound from *The Price Is Right*.

The waiting was meant to be a prep season.

As John Ortberg said, "Biblically, waiting is not just some-thing we have to do until we get what we want. Waiting is part of the process of becoming what God wants us to be."[2]

A healthy marriage is made up of healthy individuals. You may never have had a long, committed relationship, but if you prepare your character for one, you'll be more ready than you might expect. The same goes for having a child. Prepare your character for parenting, and you'll become more ready than you once were.

The training ground for your *next* is right here, where you are today. The question is, What do you want to do with it?

Rich and I once rented a home with a cracked ceiling that leaked. After examining it, a repairman said the whole AC system needed to be replaced. But our landlord insisted on simply paint-ing over the cracks.

Can you guess where this story is going?

A while later, when my brother was staying with us, he was lying in bed when the entire ceiling caved in and fell on top of him. My poor brother. Thankfully he was okay, but there cer-tainly was no hiding the need for renovation any longer. While the paint job had made it look great on the outside, it was decay-ing on the inside. And it was only a matter of time before that became obvious.

None of us wants to drift toward deterioration, but that's where neglecting our inner life will leave us. In every day of the wait, our choices will dictate our development.

Meanwhile the Spirit is calling, *Draw near. Open yourself to me. Allow me to come renovate your heart.*

The Power of Slowness

Do you remember the Aesop's fable "The Tortoise and the Hare"?

The hare is fast and boastful. The tortoise is slow but hard-working, committed to finishing what he starts. They agree to a race, and the hare takes off faster than lightning. He gets so far ahead that he even decides to take a nap. Undaunted by being left in the dust, the tortoise continues on the path, slow yet persistent. When the hare wakes up after oversleeping, he rushes forward only to see the tortoise cross the finish line ahead of him.

Slow and steady wins the race.

Patience and focus beat haste and impulsiveness.

When we find ourselves resenting the slowness of the wait, we can look around and find many reminders that worthwhile things take time.

It is not overnight that muscles develop in our bodies, or an artist paints a masterpiece, or a tiny tree expands into a fortress.

Crops grow for years before they produce fruit. Every step between cultivating the soil and bringing in the harvest requires patience, perseverance, and delayed gratification.

Whenever people create positive generational shifts, grow communities, or develop city infrastructures, it takes years, if not decades, of building—if they do it right.

The slowness isn't just the common factor here; it is one of the *key* factors.

In college I took a class on ornamental horticulture and learned about the century plant. It is small, about the size of a bush, and lives ten to thirty years at that exact size. Then there's a point when the plant starts to grow and, within a month, it stretches to twenty-eight feet tall. It gets massive!

For the first few decades, you could look at this plant and assume it would always stay that small. But you wouldn't know about the seed God had placed in it for the appointed time.

Perhaps you look at yourself and size yourself up, like I do. I probably will always be this way, fighting off thoughts like, *I'm not smart enough or pretty enough. I don't have the right education, or the right family, or enough money*—on and on. Whatever limits you see in yourself, remember, you don't know what seed God has planted in you. Have faith and it will come to fruition over time.

How many people would have looked at Jesus in his first phases of life and assumed they had him pegged? No one could have known all that God had in store. Jesus wasn't born to be a carpenter, and yet he spent decades working as one. It was preparing him.

Think of it: He spent *thirty years* living a quiet life before he began his ministry, choosing faithfulness in small ways moment after moment, day after day.

If God designed his own life on earth to be a slow burn, why wouldn't ours be?

And if Jesus embraced it, why shouldn't we do the same?

An Invitation of a Lifetime

I started this chapter telling you about the heartache of my twenty-fifth birthday. I didn't know it, but I was striking a match that day.

I was beginning a slow-burn wait that ultimately birthed more in me than any other seemingly fruitful season. It was the start of a brand-new creation in me that gave me more strength and grace for the rest of my journey.

Today, you could be in a place of heartache yourself. Even so, is it possible this is the time a brand-new creation will begin in you too?

Maybe you feel like the world is closing in on you. You could be completely at a loss of what to do next. Or perhaps you feel desperately stuck, stifled in the limitations of your current season. Any joy and zest for life seems out of reach.

While all those feelings are real, the story they're telling isn't true. Because it isn't the whole story.

God is the Author of your life, and he has goodness ahead for you. There's a story he wants to tell through you, and he isn't waiting to write it. He's writing it as you wait. Right here, right now.

God is alive, at work, and with you. He has given you an eternal soul, one that he can speak to. And the eyes of your soul can determine the story you tell yourself about your life, who you are, and what God can do.

Ask him to speak to you about where to set your eyes moving forward and to lead you into his will for you. Go ahead and dream about how he might change you in the wait.

I started as a girl overwhelmed with the medical system and afraid to advocate for myself. I tried to control the narrative and the timing. And I insisted on isolating myself from others.

But then I came to realize that God knew me better than I knew myself. I developed an honesty with him, and I dug my trust into his foundation with reckless abandon. I gained faith as I prayed with others and for others. I leaned into vulnerability, which created deep friendships and long-lasting support. And eventually the fighter in me rose up in a strength that was not my own and seized the day.

There was a deep development happening in me every single day of my journey. As I reflect, I wouldn't take back one moment—despite all the tears, failures, questions, anger, and disillusionment—because of who I became through it. When I allowed God to renew my mind, he did so much more in me than I thought possible. I found myself having a firm confidence that I was in God's will even though I was completely unable to see the outcome ahead.

There is a promised payoff for your trust in the wait. You will develop a strength, wisdom, and perseverance that will permeate every part of your life. More than anything, you will come to know God's faithfulness and character more deeply and experience his love like never before.

A season of waiting is one of the greatest invitations you will have in life. God wants to give you a pace and perspective that only come from the wait; he'll give you time to reflect, renew, and then refocus. I believe you are in your finest hour because God is close, and I have great expectation for all he desires to do in your life from the inside out.

Will you believe that the "right life for you" is delayed or that you are walking in your destiny right now?

Are you in defeat or divine design?

Are you in weakness or strength?

Are you a victim or a victor?

Is this season a burden or a blessing?

If you can't answer with certainty today, that's okay. God will grow you and build certainty in you. He will grow all kinds of things in you.

Your *next* depends on how you steward your *now*.

Strike the match and start the slow burn.

This might be the most powerful moment of your journey so far.

YOUR *NEXT* DEPENDS ON HOW YOU STEWARD YOUR *NOW*.

CHAPTER 3

Eye to Eye

The first time I held my oldest son is a moment I will never forget.

I had waited eight years to see this face, a mystery that had brought delight with each day getting closer to his birth. During delivery, when I heard his first loud baby cry, I laughed. It was a rapture of joy beyond my belief.

"He's a legend!" Rich shouted several times as Wyatt continued to exercise his lungs.

He was crying as they brought him to me, but when he heard my voice, he stopped. We knew each other. I kissed his face several times and told him I loved him.

There he was, healthy, shockingly blond, and immediately the very beat of our hearts.

I suddenly had a new hand to hold, a new face to kiss, a new voice to know, and a new laugh to miss. He would never outgrow my waiting arms.

That first night in the hospital, my husband held our son on his chest in the darkness, tears streaming down his face. "Babe, what is he doing to me?" he whispered. "This is changing everything. I love him so much."

At one point a nurse told me Wyatt could see only eight

inches in front of him. I learned that as I fed him it was the perfect distance from my face to his for him to see me. For the first few weeks, he really didn't need to see anything beyond his mother's face. Eye to eye, I cared for him, moment after moment.

You and I have a Father who longs to be eye to eye caring for us, moment after moment.

We are the children of the one who *is love*.

God so loved the world that he sent his son to stand eye to eye with us. He came to us. God didn't send him as an ethereal cloud, a majestic being, or an angel. He sent flesh and blood to look eye to eye.

He comes to where you are today:

In the unspoken loneliness you feel while trusting him with the desires of your heart.

In the complicated relationships that weigh you down no matter how hard you try to rise above.

In the unexpected struggle to find fulfillment and contentment.

In the war room of your faith as you continue to believe for a miracle or grapple with the finality of loss.

Where are you and what do you see?

Maybe you feel forgotten or far away from God, though he is always tenderly mindful of you, offering a loving assurance like no other.

He has never looked away.

His Eyes Are on You

Years ago my mother, my sister, and I were at a conference on the West Coast. We were only attending, not stepping onto the stage to speak, and enjoying just being in the faith-filled room. In one of the sessions, the host suddenly started talking about infertility and the prayer for healing, then asked every woman who was walking through infertility to stand.

My heart started to race, and I clenched my sister's jeans.

"I don't want to stand. I don't want anyone to pray for me. This is not helping me!" I pleaded.

But I had already shared my story publicly a few years earlier, so I knew I didn't really have a choice.

At the time I was feeling stable in the wait, not overcome with heartache and weariness, but this moment blindsided me. It came out of nowhere and immediately flipped my emotions. My heart wasn't ready for the instant deep dive, and it shocked my soul.

I stood, along with many other women in the wait, and received the prayer. I imagine it helped many women feel seen and supported. I also imagine there were others who did not stand because it exposed a place in them too tender and deep to share.

I have come to a place of sensitivity for people in the wait. Many times I have chosen to sit quietly instead of standing, knowing that God knows my heart and his eyes are the only eyes I need to feel on me.

Whatever we make public is still personal. Whatever we choose to share is still sacred. And as we wait, we must keep inhabiting that personal, sacred space with grace when unexpected moments surface.

You are allowed to have privacy, wherever you are on your journey. Sometimes only knowing that God knows is enough. And however healed you may be, hold on to the reality that the most tender parts of you are sacred and protected.

You are seen.

His eyes are on you.

He's Reaching Out to You

Remember that we are, after all, talking about the eyes of the Almighty. They hold much power. In Revelation, John said Jesus' eyes were "like a flame of fire" (19:12). His eyes can see deep into our souls with a purifying, refining fire. They cause conviction and transformation of the heart, as they did with Peter after his denial.

The eyes of Jesus were never too busy to spot the outcast or those on the periphery of the immediate objective. He saw Martha in her hurry, Nathaniel under the fig tree, and perceived the motivations of his critics, discerning their hearts from afar.[1]

Jesus employed his sight as he healed the deaf and mute man, looking up to heaven before the miracle transpired. He looked at a crowd with compassion, knowing they were wandering helpless and blind. And his gaze was full of love as he looked at the rich young ruler, a man deceived by his own self-righteousness and lost in his search for truth.[2]

Eighteen years ago, when Rich and I had been married only a few months and were starting the adventure of our life, I moved from Tennessee to Miami. I am directionally challenged in a small town, let alone a metropolis, so my first solo trip to South Beach was memorable to say the least.

In the middle of the August heat, I ran out of gas in a neighborhood I had never been in; I couldn't even recall how I got there. Rich was unavailable so, in a panic, I called my friend David, who worked on South Beach. In a rush I explained my predicament, then sputtered, "I don't know what to do! Would you be able to help me?"

"Where are you?" he asked.

"I don't know!" I answered with urgency. "All I see is this big white building with strange circle windows."

"I know exactly where you are," he replied, to my relief. "Hang tight and I'll be there soon."

Thank God for good friends.

I have good news: Our God is better than a good friend. You may be so lost that you can't even describe your surroundings—but all you need to do is admit that you're lost and he will come running. It's what he did through Jesus; we were lost, so he came to us.

God has a perfect track record. He always shows up. He'll leave the ninety-nine sheep to rescue the one wandering. As we just saw in Scripture, time after time in Jesus' life on earth, he sought out the ones in need.

His eyes keep careful watch over you now, interceding for you at the right hand of the Father, omniscient and invested in your every moment.

In the slow burn, you are seen and you are known.

Yes, He'll Come to You Even *There*

There may be days when you hear all this and think, *Maybe God can see me and know me. But my life is a wreck right now. My story isn't pretty. I am too much of a mess for anyone to reach me.*

And if you listen closely, you might hear God reply, *Try me.*

Well, I'm feeling really hopeless, you might say. *I'm in the darkest place of my life.*

That's how the woman with the issue of blood felt.[3] She was suffering with a disease as well as a sense of futility. There is nothing more discouraging than nothing working—to try everything and see everything fail. Today if you feel helpless, God comes to you where you are.

Maybe you'd tell God instead, *I'm in a dead-end place that feels wrong. I'm at a loss about how to change or who I'm supposed to be.*

If you had asked Peter, "Who are you?" he would have said, "Are you kidding me? Like I have a choice. Generation after generation, my people have been fishermen. It's not like there's a job fair around here. I'm just a fisherman; that is all I'll ever do."

Then Jesus came to Peter and spoke to his limitation. Talk about lifting the ceiling off his life! It's as if Jesus was speaking to Peter's heart, saying "You have no idea yet who you will become. I'm telling you, you will be a *fisher of men*."[4] Today, if you feel stuck and you don't know what's next, God comes to where you are.

I'm drowning in the weight of shame, you might say. *I've blown it so many times and there's no excuse for where I am at in my life at this point.*

The woman at the well was debilitated by shame, and the first words Jesus said to her revealed his interest in her quality of life. Using the powerful metaphor of water, he let her know he could replenish her dehydrated soul.[5] So many of us find ourselves here. If that's you today, he comes to you right where you are.

My life is chaos, you might say.

When the disciples were on a boat in a storm at night, feeling beaten, the violent wind and waves threatened to overcome them. They could barely see anything before their eyes, let alone the possibility of survival. But Jesus walked on water to get to them and protect them.[6] However chaotic your life might be today, he comes to where you are.

I'm haunted by my trauma, you might say. *Its grip on me is unrelenting and it's controlling my life.*

There once was a man who was bound by darkness; he was possessed by a demon and living among tombs. Jesus came to him in his torment and misery.[7] Sometimes we forget that whenever the Light goes eye to eye with the darkness, the Light always overtakes it. You may be living among the tombs of your past, your torment, your pain. If you are, he comes to where you are.

There is no place he won't go to reach you, the child he loves. He proved that when he came to earth as man, meeting people in their messes, connecting directly to their need. He came not to a palace but to a stable. Not to royalty but to a teenage virgin. Not as a king but as a servant.

He is right there with you as you read these words, ready to look you in the eyes and say, *You are not alone.*

He Will Meet Your Deepest Needs

Jesus not only comes to where you are; he also comes as *who you need.*

While I love my husband deeply, I can't always sense what his heart needs. No matter how many years we spend with someone, we can never fully know the depths and reach of their thoughts and desires.

But does this stop me from thinking I know what Rich is trying to say in any given conversation? No. It's a big joke in our home that I'm the incorrigible interrupter. If Rich even slightly pauses while speaking, I'll feel confident I know exactly where he's headed, so I'll try to help him out and finish his sentences. Besides annoying Rich like crazy, it honestly gets hysterical how off I am at times. For instance, at a restaurant I'll look at him and think, *He wants to leave,* when it turns out he's thinking, *I want dessert.*

A version of this plays out with my kids too; I can't always tell what they need.

Now, they've got three different cries—hungry, sleepy, dirty diaper—and those I've got down cold.

Hungry is really *hangry*; the sound here is like a low guttural growl.

Sleepy is a full-on meltdown. Bottom lip out, eyebrows furrowed, tears streaming. *You blew it, Mom. I'm exhausted, so now I refuse to sleep.*

Dirty diaper is a ticked-off shout, full volume. *Hello! I can't walk myself to the changing table. Going to need your legs, Mom!*

But sometimes they do a new thing, and I have no idea what they want. What's crazy is, I will pay such close attention and try my hardest to read them right and still get it wrong.

News flash: Your God will not get it wrong. He doesn't have to play a guessing game with you. He knows what you need!

When he sees you in need, he will show up. Always.

And when he shows up, he won't be just a complacent bystander. He will empower you and supply you. He will encourage you and cheer you on.

The problem is this: What we need is not always what we want. So while God knows our need, we do not.

What you want is a prophetic word from the stage; what you need is to shut yourself away and hear him speak.

What you want is twenty-year vision; what you need is to read your Bible today.

What you want is a big position leading many; what you need is to serve where you are. What you want is a deep, intimate relationship; what you need is a whole and healed heart.

What you want is a new job; what you need is a new attitude.

God came to humanity in a way that met their true need. What the people wanted was a flashy king on an earthly throne; what they needed was a Savior who could show them God's heart.

He knew they needed not only to receive forgiveness for their sins but also to see his perfect love within a human so that we, too, could love with his love. And he knows the same is true for you and me.

Seeing All That You Can

When he comes to us and we look at him, what do we see?

If it's not clear, we can let Scripture guide us. It describes God in human terms, making references to things we can grasp, even though God's nature goes beyond what our minds can fathom.

He is the sun, the light, the day, and the morning star. He is fire, a torch, a fountain, and a rock. He's a shield, a hiding place, a shadow, and a temple. An eagle, a lion, and a hen.

All of creation indeed sings of his glory!

Scripture also refers to God as the Bridegroom and a husband. He's a shepherd, a potter, and a physician. A king and a man of war. He is the Lord, mighty in power!

We also see our own human emotions and abilities mirrored in descriptions of him. We read that he is knowing, seeing, and remembering; he's smelling and tasting; he's sitting, rising, walking, sleeping, and wiping away tears.

And then there are many names of God, which speak to his personal interactions with humanity and reflect the redemptive story. His names are all paths to our hearts.

The name of the Lord is a strong tower. We can run to it and find shelter.

He's the Healer for our wounds and brokenness.

The Provider for our lack.

A Father to the fatherless and those with father issues.

The Prince of Peace when we are in chaos.

The Lord of light who overcomes the darkness in our lives.

The Deliverer when we are in bondage.

The Savior when we are stuck helpless in a pit.

We can call him *Jehovah Machsi*, meaning, "the Lord my refuge."

Or *Jehovah Nissi*, "the Lord my banner."

Or *Peleh Yo'etz*, "wonderful Counselor."

Our God is the Alpha and Omega. The first and the last. The beginning and the end. All of this is only a glimpse, a taste, a shadow, an impression of the magnitude of his nature.

This is the God who comes to meet you. He whispers to your heart, *Will you look closer and come to know more of who I am?*

In the slow burn, you come to see more and more of the Savior.

One day shortly after Wyatt was born, I stepped out of my house for a walk for the first time after coming home from the hospital. It had been painful to even sit up after the C-section and I asked my dad to walk around our neighborhood with Wyatt and me as the sun was setting. I had slept so little and spent days in my bedroom, so just getting out of my pajamas and breathing fresh air was rejuvenating.

As I looked around and took in the purple- and pink-laced sky, my heart whispered to me, *There is so much more.* I thought of newborn Wyatt seeing only eight inches in front of him, unaware of the vast landscape beyond that. But his limited sight did not limit reality.

So it is with us. There is so much more beyond our view. Are you willing to believe that there is more than you currently can see in your marriage and your home? In your purpose and across the landscape of your life? Who are we to think that in our short time on the planet, that in our finiteness, we have seen all there is? You live under an open sky. God is all around you.

And he has promised that no eye has seen, nor ear has heard what he has prepared for those that love him.[8]

There are times our sight feels limited like Wyatt's, only

seeing eight inches in front of us. I lived in the eight inches for eight years. But even in the eight inches I was eye to eye with God.

If you are in pain, disappointed, or feel rejected, know that a loving God is waiting to help you. Will you choose to focus on the unclear surroundings or the clarity of your Savior? Will you choose to focus on the uncertainty or the closeness of the friend who sticks closer than a brother?

He's not far away from you today. He's eye to eye with you. He's close to you now like he was with the woman who was bleeding, with Peter, with the woman at the well, with the disciples in the storm, and with the tormented man. He came for you. Your life is as significant as every encounter you read in the pages of God's Word.

You can be like David, who said things like this to God: "Keep me as the apple of your eye; hide me in the shadow of your wings" (Psalm 17:8). He meant, "Guard me like you would your own eye and protect me." *The Message* interprets it this way: "Keep your eye on me; hide me under your cool wing feathers."

David prayed this with full assurance that his loving Father would.

God's eyes are toward you; his ears hear you; his heart is for you. He has made this abundantly clear.

His question to you is, *Do you see me today? Do you want me close?*

Keeping "First Love" Eye Contact

Waylon, my three-year-old daughter, loves to crawl into my lap and hold me close. She'll fully lock her eyes on mine, unconcerned by anything or anyone else. She'll remain in that place of closeness, not looking away, not ready to leave. Five minutes will go by. Then ten. I'll coolly suggest she go play or see another family member, but she won't entertain it for a second.

Let them wait, her stare seems to say. *I'm with you.*

At night when I put her to sleep, she often will say softly, "Mommy, lay with me," and I will lay down. She will ask for story after story, then a story-song, then a lullaby.

When our routine is done, she pats the pillow beside her and says, "I want your head right here."

If I turn my head away from her, she'll quickly say, "I want to see your face," then press her nose to mine. No fear of personal space, just warmth of complete love. She'll wrap her arm around my neck and place her feet into my tummy softly. This is how she loves to fall asleep, as close as she can possibly get to me.

This girl's heart is completely devoted to me and has been since she was born. Sure, I know she'll mature and create other friendships and meaningful connections, but right here and now, I am her sun, moon, and stars. I have never known a love like this, and neither has she.

I am her first love, the beautiful creation of parent-child connection that comes from the heart of the Father.

In Revelation, when Jesus addressed a church that had turned away from him, he said, "Return to me, your first love" (2:4–5, paraphrased). Some may think of teenage love as first love. While there is a certain kind of beauty to it with all its angst and emotion, I don't think of it that way. For me, "first love" is Waylon smashing her nose to mine, completely secure in my love, unapologetic eye contact, and dismissal of every other possibility. Abandoning everything else for my presence. There's so much more to discover in the slow-burn purpose of her life, so many more seasons and lessons to come, but she knows love now.

She doesn't have to wait. And my love for her is more than she could ever fathom.

How much more the love of our perfect God, creator and sustainer of life?

Return to me, your first love.

Hebrews 12:2 tells us to fix our eyes on Jesus, the author and finisher of our faith. And A. W. Tozer wrote, "Faith is the gaze of a soul upon a saving God."[9]

When we make eye contact, our souls are transformed.

But developing the eyes to see him truly is a slow burn. The way the eyes of our heart develop actually mirror the way our physical eyes do.

The formation of the eye within the womb is a miraculous and elaborate slow burn. Around three weeks after conception, the optic pits form; at five weeks the lens and cornea begin developing. At two months the eyelids take shape and fuse together, guarding the development taking place within. The eyes remain closed until the end of the second trimester. Throughout the final stretch of pregnancy, rapid eye movement and sleep patterns develop and the pupil light reflex matures. Development after birth continues until up to four years of age, when the retina fully evolves.[10]

It's not overnight; it's a slow burn of sight.

What's also interesting is that we see only black and white for about the first four months after birth. Slowly the colors start to come in as our sight transitions from grayscale to a rainbow of colors we are able to discern.[11] It takes time.

When we give our lives to Jesus, our first response can be to set hard, black-and-white boundaries. Our newborn eyes need defined lines to see what is good and what is bad. And if we aren't careful, we can hard-line everyone, turning relationship into religion.

God's plan for your sight is to fully develop you, not overnight but over time. God's grace allows us to mature daily as we trust him, understanding the complexities that make up life. We still see boundary lines, but, as we mature, they are multi-faceted and rich in depth. It would be a mistake to declare that only black and white exist because that's all you see right now, when God is going to bring more depth and insight over time to your vision.

Waiting allows God to mature you and show you that there are always new dimensions in your faith.

> WAITING ALLOWS GOD TO MATURE YOU AND SHOW YOU THAT THERE ARE ALWAYS NEW DIMENSIONS IN YOUR FAITH.

And all throughout the slow burn, he is developing the eyes of your heart, helping you better sense his love and nearness, forming an instinct to reach out to him. To rely on him. To feel connected to him.

In the early morning my little girl will climb into my bed wanting to cuddle and play peek-a-boo under the covers. Whenever I go and get her a new bottle, I'll return to find her hiding under the covers waiting to be discovered. I'll pull the covers back, and she'll laugh hysterically.

Yesterday I looked at her sweetly and said, "I've got my eye on you!"

To which she responded with her little voice, slowly learning to string sentences together, "Yoooou got yuuh eye on meeee."

It so touched me. She agreed it was true and rehearsed the reality out loud. She personalized it.

It's one thing for me to remind you of the promise that God guides us with his eye, but the power is when you personalize the promise and carry it with you daily.

Waylon knows she is my delight. She knows she is seen. The delight of a child knowing that full attention and care is completely focused, missing nothing. God longs for you to have this kind of relationship with him.

Even when you feel like hiding, running, or disappearing, his love is ready to wrap you up. Because of his heart for you, you can feel safe and secure knowing that you're seen and perfectly loved in every season. You can lift your eyes to the heavens with a smile and confidently say to your Creator, "You've got your eye on me!"

CHAPTER 4

Sow in the Dark

"What's your name again? Don? Cherry? Cher?"

"I'm sorry—I've never heard that name. Is it Dawn? Sherri?"

"Is there a nickname you go by that's easier?"

When people encounter my name for the first time, they've usually got questions. I've heard them all.

How is it pronounced? *Don-shur-ee.*

Where did it come from? The short answer is my one-in-a-million parents who are die-hard creatives.

The long answer goes like this: My parents, Denny and DeAnza, deliberated whether to name me Dawn (my dad's vote) or Cheré (my mom's choice). On the day I was born, they were still undecided and, as they continued to discuss it, my dad fell asleep on the couch. In true DeAnza fashion, my mom wrote a note "on behalf of" one-day-old me—a love letter to a father from his newborn baby girl—and tucked it under my dad's pillow. The note revealed my given name for the very first time, and it was literally a creative collaboration of both of my creators.

The name DawnCheré means "sunrise sweetheart." One definition phrased it as "love as faithful as the coming dawn."[1] That sounds about as romantic as it gets. And yet it alludes to

39

those moments before we see the dawn coming, when the darkness might have us convinced that we are all alone. *If you need a rescue, it won't come. If you need reassurance or support, it won't be there.* We wonder if the sun will ever rise again. But, in time, we start to see the light shine and illuminate the life surrounding us. It was there all along.

Love, God's faithful love, proves itself time and time again.

The story God has for you and me is one of waiting and finding love as faithful as the dawn—even while we are still in the dark. It is love that meets you in the dark and also brings the light.

Sometimes we are in the dark with the pain of life, feeling the impact of the illness or job loss, the betrayal or broken relationship. Other times we are feeling abandoned by God, in "the dark night of the soul," as spiritual mystics like Saint John of the Cross and Saint Teresa of Avila wrote of.[2] Disconnected and confused, they'd lost a sense of meaning and searched to find their path once again.

This spiritual depression is an invitation to die to our ego, and surrendering it can lead to transformation and connectedness not reliant on circumstances. As painful as the season is, it gives us an opportunity to assess our priorities and values and move toward purification and growth. And as the darkness lifts, we see God forming in us a new sense of purpose and deeper trust in him.

Do you feel as if you are in the dark? Maybe you feel alone, forgotten, and cold today. Hear me when I tell you that loneliness is based on a lie, one that darkness can sell to your soul like nothing else can. Even so, I know from experience that it feels true, and you'll likely have moments you wonder if the light will ever shine again.

I assure you it will.

And until then, God won't let any pain or shadow be wasted. He will make it possible for you to say one day what T. S. Eliot did: "The darkness declares the glory of light."[3] In his goodness, he will make the darkness purposeful.

How to Live in the Dark

So the big question is, What will you do in the dark? Will you sow the seeds you have?

Seeds of faith.

Seeds of obedience.

Seeds of trust.

The night is the perfect time to sow them because they can germinate without any light. In fact, seeds often grow most effectively in the dark and can even be hindered by light.

A method of growing rhubarb called "forcing" is an extreme version of this. Farmers leave the sown soil in complete darkness, which eventually forces the stalks to search upward for the light in order to grow chlorophyl. The resulting development occurs at such an accelerated pace that you actually can *hear* the rhubarb growing, the creaking or popping as cells divide in real time.[4] You hear it, but of course you can't see it, because it is happening in the dark.

The most treasured "fruit" in your life will often grow in the darkest season. As you reach for the light with full focus, you're experiencing a deep transformation. Remember that the soil of your soul is much more important than the soil of your circumstance.

As a historian and monk, Saint Bede the Venerable lived a hidden life during the Dark Ages. In his solitude he generated works that changed his culture and that people went on to study centuries after his time. In AD 731 Saint Bede completed *The Ecclesiastical History of the English People,* which detailed the spread of Christianity and the establishment of the church. Earning the name "Father of English History," he helped revive education during the early middle ages.[5]

THE MOST TREASURED "FRUIT" IN YOUR LIFE WILL OFTEN GROW IN THE DARKEST SEASON.

Living largely unseen for years in an era labeled "dark," Saint Bede's inner life still thrived as he poured energy into producing something good.

Could it be that the constraints of his life situation became a driver for his development?

Could the constraints in your life serve as a driver for you?

Don't let the sense of darkness limit the possibilities of your season. There is much within your reach right here, right now. What you choose to sow in the night will take root and later bring a harvest in the light of day.

But what about when we feel so broken that all we have to "sow" are tears?[d]

Receive the reassuring words of Psalm 126: "Those who sow in tears shall reap with shouts of joy! [S]he who goes out weeping, bearing the seed for sowing, shall come home with shouts of joy, bringing [her] sheaves with [her]" (vv. 5–6).

Here is a promise to hold on to in the dark! God says our tears are our seeds to sow and our season of sorrow will not last forever. The psalmist described eruptive joy and bountiful *sheaves*—bundles of harvested grain stalks, the result of much effort and patience.

What is the emotion we reap? *Joy.*

---

d. See appendix for the handwritten journal entry.

Hannah sowed tears of trust and honesty. David sowed tears of repentance as he wept for the sins he had committed against God. The woman with the alabaster box sowed tears of adoration and worship.

The common reality among them? They all eventually reaped their harvest with a heart of joy. "Weeping may stay for the night, but rejoicing comes in the morning" (Psalm 30:5 NIV).

One morning in 2016, I called my grandmother to catch up. She had lost the love of her life, my grandfather, a few years earlier and it had been a devastating season. Sixty-three years of marriage to a delightful, strong, and faithful man and then several years of being fully on her own.

That day, however, Grammy sounded better than ever; I could sense the joy in her voice over the phone. For several months she had been spending the early hours of every day in prayer with Jesus and had recently found herself telling him, "Lord, I'm happy. I never expected to be happy. I expected only to get by after Rodney's death, but I'm doing better than that. I am truly happy."

I cried as I listened to her say this. She had married Papa when she was only sixteen; life with him was all she'd known for decades. And yet God had given her a new breath of life for a new season. At almost ninety years old, Grammy knew she was not alone. Her Father God had faithfully stayed close to her. She knew the deep joy of his nearness. She was still his little girl, and he was still her wonderful Father, forever comforting, loving, and leading.

Grammy had sown her tears and entrusted them to God long enough to reap them with shouts of joy. The season that had seemed to offer only the chance to endure surprisingly brought the miracle of new mercies.

I know there were days she didn't feel like sowing—to come

to God with her heartache and struggle, with her trust and obedience. It would have been easier to hold on to her seeds and wait to have faith until the sun was shining and she could see everything clearly. But she didn't do that. Why? Because she knew that it is only by sowing that the state of our hearts can begin to change.

C. S. Lewis wrote, "Holy places are dark places. It is life and strength, not knowledge and words, that we get in them."[6]

As we come to him with our open hearts and full trust, he will do what only he can.

When Tears Fall

When I was in tenth grade, I developed Bell's palsy, which permanently paralyzed one of my tear ducts. It first manifested one night when I was sitting around the dinner table with our family of eight. Mid-conversation, I saw a look of horror come over my mom's face. I hadn't realized it, but one side of my face had suddenly become completely paralyzed, mid-bite of spaghetti and meatballs. My eye, cheek, and lip drooped involuntarily.

Our doctor told us more about the condition over the phone that night, and we started to learn what to expect. My symptoms persisted for several weeks, then it was over. While it's been decades since it happened, I still have lasting side effects. One is that, from time to time, my left eye will release a stream of tears with no warning.

But this physical condition isn't the only reason tears will sometimes sneak up on me. Have you had those moments too? When we're going through a dark season, our heart is often especially tender and the tears can spring up out of nowhere.

Think about that word *tender*. This is the sensitive state of the heart in times of deep need.

Maybe you're tender every time you think of a desperate need in your family. Or you're feeling tender brokenness from a severe disappointment. You might have an aching, silent fear of what could happen if a problem you face persists. Or you're tender with a deep longing for a miracle. If you're in a place where only God can do what is needed, he has met you here. And his heart is tender toward you.

Romans 8:24–25 says, "In this hope we were saved. But hope that is seen is no hope at all. Who hopes for what they already have? But if we hope for what we do not yet have, we *wait* for it patiently" (NIV).

If you will wait, he will work.

Paul went on to say that even when believers don't have the words to say, the Holy Spirit interprets their groans and sighs.

IF YOU WILL WAIT, HE WILL WORK.

God is deciphering your every breath, ache, and tear—and he isn't guessing. He *knows*.

Without a word, you can sow your tears today in full surrender. So lay your burdens down. Allow the tenderness you can't escape to pull you closer to his heart than you've ever been before. His heart is tender toward you. Let him hold you and bring a harvest.

Let It Flow

Perhaps your tears are desert-dry today and have been for years. The disconnect between how you feel and your ability to express it is numbing your soul and has made your heart feel like stone. Or perhaps you grew up in a home that rejected expression of emotion, and the thought of tears is foreign and unnerving.

My husband wrote a song called "Let It Flow," and its lyrics are profound.

Sometimes my tears are oceans
Sometimes they're desert dry
But you hold my every moment
So what do I have to hide
If everything's in your sight?
So let it flow, let it flow.
From the depths of my soul.
'Cause I know
When I'm broken, you are close.

Every tear from my eyes
Every season of my life
I lift you high
Thank God you hear my cry
All of my tears recorded
Yet all of my sins are not
Who is this God of mercy?
So what do I have to hide
If everything's in your sight?

My soul waits for the Lord
Forever and ever.[7]

In this moment, ask God to help you entrust the pain to him, to no longer hold on to the tears but sow them into his safe and able hands.

What is the power of our tears? Tears tell. Tears translate. Tears release and tears cleanse. What the tongue cannot express, tears tell. What no language can adequately describe, tears translate. What the heart cannot contain, tears release. What water cannot wash, tears cleanse. Tears of joy, grief, confusion, frustration, and relief.

"Jesus wept," Scripture tells us (John 11:35). It's a powerful statement revealing a Savior acquainted with our grief. The strongest man in history knew that surrendering his tears to the Father only made him stronger.

In a sense, his tears were a war cry. And yours can be too.

After Jesus wept, he defeated the grave and redeemed every tear he had shed as Lazarus walked out of his grave.

After Jesus wept, he drank the cup of pain, enduring the cross for the glory set before him, and defeated the Enemy of darkness with one final sacrifice for all mankind. It was a war cry—a signal of a new beginning, not the end. It wasn't the finality of defeat; it was the certainty of victory.

Don't mistake your tears as the final harvest of grief. No, friend, they are seeds, and every drop is an expression of faith in a God who redeems all.

This is the God who declares, "I will open rivers on the bare heights, and fountains in the midst of the valleys. I will make the wilderness a pool of water, and the dry land springs of water" (Isaiah 41:18).

A national park in California illustrates this well. Ominously named Death Valley, it is the lowest, hottest, and driest area in North America. Talk about a slow burn. It's obviously not a spot you'd expect to see much flourishing. But every ten to fifteen years, a remarkable phenomenon occurs: A vast number of wildflowers bloom simultaneously, creating stunning landscapes filled with vibrant colors. It's called a *superbloom*. The dormant seeds germinate as the rain falls in winter months, taking the soil from slow burn to superbloom in one supernatural season.[8]

Wherever we find ourselves, and no matter how many tears fall, we can keep putting our hope in the God who knows how to create a surprise superbloom in a dry place.

The Tear Keeper

Whether we're constantly feeling exposed with raw tenderness or we are working toward self-awareness and vulnerability, God sees exactly where we are. He knows our hearts better than we do. And he is with us.

"Is there anyplace I can go to avoid your Spirit? To be out of your sight?" David asked God. "If I climb to the sky, you're there! . . . Then I said to myself, 'Oh, he even sees me in the dark!' . . . You know me inside and out" (Psalm 139:7–8, 11, 13 MSG). In every moment of our lives, he understands us. In every place, he is with us, surrounding us with compassion and love.

"You keep track of all my sorrows," David also wrote. "You have collected all my tears in your bottle. You have recorded each one in your book" (Psalm 56:8 NLT). The ancient practice of collecting tears in a small bottle was a cultural act of remembrance for the grieving. David reflected on the tenderness of a God who catches every tear of his children, valuable and remembered.

It is as if our Father is saying, *My beloved child, do not assume you are alone in your sorrow or that I will soon forget it. And do not bottle up your emotions inside yourself; release them to me and to the safe place I have for them. Come closer and feel my love as you're aching.*

The Father holds our tears because our tears are an intimate and indispensable part of the personal relationship we have with him. Conversation is not always in a language we know; sometimes we say more without a word than we can even comprehend. Tears translate what our heart cannot explain. And so, he keeps every one in his bottle and in his book. Because he loves us. Every drop released from the levee of our soul lands in the hands that hold oceans.

He has the tears I have hidden. The ones I have wiped away.

The ones that have stained journal pages, blue jeans, pillowcases, and red-carpeted altars. He treasures them all. My pain is held in his bottle. My confusion, disillusionment, anger, and heart wounds, all wrestled out with tears that escaped my eyes in full surrender.

One after another, they are messages in a bottle—tears that say, *I trust you, Jesus.*

I need you.

I feel you.

I seek you.

I love you.

My tears are a fluency that only God fully understands. They flow in the deepest parts of my heart that only he knows.

The same goes for you. The stream of tears that once fell on rosy young cheeks will later fall on wrinkled ones, always flowing on a well-worn path from your heart to your Father's heart. To the one who knows you better than you know yourself and loves you more than anyone else ever could.

Hear me when I tell you today that you are perfectly loved. Every part of you is cherished and valued. Not by what you create, achieve, or prove. An aspect of God's love for you is knowing you fully and treasuring you for *who you are*. He is the only one who knows the extent of your worth because he gave it to you.

Augustine said of God, "You are good and all-powerful, caring for each one of us as though the only one in your care, and yet for all as for each individual."[9]

And Tim Keller wrote, "The only love that won't disappoint you is one that can't change, that can't be lost, that is not based on the ups and downs of life or how well you live. It is something that not even death can take away from you. God's love is the only thing like that."[10]

Rich and I were in a season of pain a few years ago after losing a friend to cancer. As we were grieving, I penned this simple chorus to Jesus. I pictured him sitting with me, listening and leaning in. Weeping with me and reminding me that the dawn is breaking.

> *Come cry with me.*
> *You can count my tears.*
> *I'll tell you everything.*
> *After all these years*
> *You're still the one I need.*
> *Without a word you speak*
> *When you cry with me.*[e]

Your tears are a gift from your Creator to communicate what your language and intellect cannot.

The next time a tear creeps up and escapes without permission, or you notice the currents of desperation underlying your daily moments, make that moment an altar. Right then. Right there. You don't have to say a word. Every tear and every ache speak inexpressibly. Sow them all today in full surrender. Let them flow. Lay your burdens down.

If you're numb, may he give you a heart of flesh for a heart of stone.

If you feel incapable of entrusting your heart, may God meet you right where you are and reveal his faithfulness.

And if you are tender, may the tenderness you can't escape pull you closer than you've ever been to his heart.

Wherever you are, he is with you and his heart is tender toward you. Let him hold you and bring a harvest.

---

e. See appendix for the handwritten journal entry.

CHAPTER 5

Calling the Warrior Within

Sometimes warriors hide in bathrooms before they find their strength.

I was fourteen years old and living my best life in Shreveport, Louisiana. I had wonderful friends, a great school, and weekends full of bonfires and Friday night football. Most days you would find me smiling—except on some Sundays, when my dad would, without warning, call me up to the front of the church to sing before or after his sermon. I loved to sing; that was not the problem. The problem was the people. All of them. Staring at me.

I would nervously grasp the mic and combat a million insecure thoughts in my head as I eked out each note. My fear was like a cage that imprisoned me and made me live small. I eventually came up with reasons to get out of service. "I have to go pick up my brothers from kids' church." Or, "I need to go help with something urgent upstairs." Even hiding in a bathroom stall for twenty minutes toward the end of the service was a safe bet. For a while, it worked for me. I was able to cope with my fear through these careful strategies of self-protection.

Remember how my entire family is musical? My dad wrote a Christmas musical that we performed annually, and he was always developing it year after year. When I was fourteen, we'd booked a full week of ten blockbuster performances at the historic Strand Theatre. Leading up to it, my dad came home one day and announced, "DC, I just wrote a song for you! You'll sing it at *Songs of the Season*. It's called 'He'll Be There for You.'"

I suddenly went pale and, without thinking, blurted, "I can't do that, Dad. I'm afraid." It was my honest reaction, the only perspective that felt possible.

My dad is not a bully. But in that moment he spoke the truth that challenged me. Without raising his voice, he spoke to my heart in a way that felt like a shout: "DawnChéré, if you don't step into what God is calling you to, he will use someone else."

For this girl, who always wanted to earn an A+, those words felt crushing. I ran up to my room and sat on my yellow plaid comforter. The thought *I have disappointed God* and the words *He will use someone else* echoed in my mind as I cried.

Before long, my mom walked into my room and sat beside me on my bed as I wept quietly.

After a while she said, "DawnChéré, your dad is not mad at you. He's speaking to the warrior inside you, calling you to stand up and fight."[f]

As badly as I wanted my parents to say, "She's just too young," and give me a hall pass, to choose someone else to sing and give me another year to be ready, I knew they had both called my bluff.

A few months before, we had been at a funeral where the grieving widow had requested that I sing, and—again—I'd hid in my dad's office, cried in fear, and made my mom cover for me. Fear was controlling my mind and limiting my life.

The self-consciousness was so intense that it restricted my view, making my world all about me. I couldn't see that my gift wasn't for me; it was for God to use. I wasn't meant to hide it away

---

f. See appendix for the handwritten journal entry.

while doubting myself; I was meant to give it away, openhandedly offering it to God and the world around me. I couldn't consider others' needs when I was caught in a self-centered stronghold of what others might think of me and preoccupied with not being perfect.

On top of all of this, I was ashamed of my stinginess, my inability to give what I could to others, and tired of feeling like I couldn't participate in community.

I had been stuck in a miserable place for a long while when I heard those words, *"DawnCheré ... he's speaking to the warrior inside you."*

And that day, I decided to stand up and fight.

The words of my parents weren't just words; they were a charge to the depths of my soul. I was delaying the destiny of God because I was waiting to feel ready. But courage comes from obedience. And my obedience to step out, even willing to be a fool, was met with strength from heaven and a new perspective of ministering to others instead of impressing them.

While my newfound resolve may have appeared instantaneous, God had been working patiently in my heart for years to bring me to that moment of surrender. It had been a raw wrestle of my faith and fear as I vacillated between feeling throttled by fear and choosing to trust God again and again.

Even today, it continues to be a slow burn of obedience and trust in my life. I make a daily sacrifice of prayer and worship, laying down my fear on the altar and letting it bring a fragrant offering to God.

Months after I decided to "stand up and fight," I had another moment with God at a weekend retreat that marks my life today. While kneeling at the altar, I released my fear and told God I would trust and obey. I didn't know what t but at the closing of the retreat, there was testim

"Who wants to share?" the leader asked the group. Sharing in public was the last thing I wanted to do, yet something in me had changed. It wasn't that I wanted to say something; it's that I had something to say.

I raised my hand, and when they handed me the mic, I shared the amazing things I'd seen our God do. He had done a work in me, and it was like a river that flowed out of my heart and a fire that burned in my spirit. It consumed me—and it consumed my fear. My perspective had changed.

I'm not just talking; I'm reporting. I'm witnessing, I realized.

I'm willing to look like a fool. I'm willing to be the only one. I'm willing to share what I have found. His presence is alive and active in me.

Eugene Peterson once wrote, "I don't want to end up a bureaucrat in the time-management business for God or a librarian cataloging timeless truths. Salvation is kicking in the womb of creation right now, any time now. Pay attention."[1] You are not simply reporting what has happened in the past. You are a real-time reporter telling of a living God doing miraculous wonders.

Because of where I have walked, I know this for sure: Fear will steal your offering. But you don't have to let it. The warrior inside you can fight it off and protect what matters.

Choosing to Triumph over Fear

Nelson Mandela faced tremendous fear when he stood against apartheid, a racial segregation policy in South Africa that lasted for decades. He fought through his fear so he could keep pushing back on the discriminating system. Mandela was unjustly arrested for his activism and imprisoned for twenty-seven years before he saw South Africa experience freedom. I can only imagine how he felt during those twenty-seven years of waiting, wondering if he would ever be vindicated or see justice in his country.

Mandela went on to become the first Black president of South Africa, helping to unify a deeply divided nation instead of seeking revenge. His courage to fight fear and his willingness to wait led to incredible political change and generational impact. He famously declared, "I learned that courage was not the absence of fear, but the triumph over it."[2]

How many of us would do the same? When fear reigns in us, it leaves us in a prison of waiting with no hope of release. We start to believe the intimidating thoughts of the Enemy that come into our head—and if we continue in that vein, we will never be ready for what God is calling us to.

While I cannot say I would have been as bold or patient as Mandela, one of the most important things I have learned in my life is to guard my mind. I have developed a practice of evicting thoughts of fear; I don't even let them take up space. When they try to "enter the room," I shift my thoughts in another direction. It is a topic worthy of an entire discussion, one we'll have later in chapter 7.

Sometimes we are in the grip of fear without naming it. Maybe we are stagnant, and we label it *waiting* when in fact we are hiding. Have you ever been there? Deep in your heart you hold dynamic, beautiful dreams, but you can't break out of your own chains of insecurity and self-doubt. You might be able to see there is plenty to be done now, but you just can't seem to push through the fear. Where can you begin? How?

I imagine Moses was asking those same kinds of questions before he found himself speaking with God at the burning bush in Exodus 3.

Nothing Has to Hold You Back

Moses had been in exile from Egypt, living in the desert—a seemingly never-ending wait. He had run away from his home after murdering an Egyptian slave master; the Hebrew people, who he'd been trying to help, held it against him in contempt. The very people he was trying to save were the people that made him run from Egypt in fear.

He'd been hiding away for forty years, trying to live a simple life, when God sought him out and called him by name. God suddenly came from heaven to earth to get Moses' attention and tell him that he would be the one to lead God's people out of slavery in Egypt.

"From within the bush," God called him by name: "Moses! Moses!" (Exodus 3:4 NIV).

Today, God calls you by name.

You may have ignored him the first time or wasted away the last few years—but today, as you read this, hear heaven call you by name once more. Now is the time to say, "Here I am."

Why don't you say that right now in your heart as you are reading? *Here I am.*

The first thing to do in a God moment is respond. You don't have to pull all the pieces together or fix yourself up. Even your waiting in the desert that seemed like a lost season has prepared you for this moment. Notice that Moses' biggest mission didn't begin until he was eighty years old. Were his first eight decades a waste? Or was God preparing him to change history?

Sometimes waiting feels like wandering, a feeling Moses knew well as he spent forty years on the back side of a desert. We know Moses dealt with fear—that he wasn't worthy, that he'd be ineffective, that no one would follow him. He had no reference or ability to even comprehend what God was about to do through him. But it all transpired in the third phase of his life, which tells me that you don't have to fear that God can't use you, and there is no telling what God has in store for you next.

You're not late today.

Sam Walton opened up the first Walmart when he was forty-four years old. Martha Stewart launched *Martha Stewart Living* at age forty-nine. J. R. R. Tolkien published his first novel, *The Hobbit*, at forty-five and finished publishing *The Lord of the Rings* at sixty-three. John Warnock founded Adobe at age forty-two and launched the revolutionary format of Portable Document Format (PDF) when he was fifty-two.

John B. Fenn won a Nobel Prize for his work in chemistry in his eighties. Grandma Moses started painting in her seventies and her work didn't find great success until her eighties. And Harland Sanders founded Kentucky Fried Chicken at sixty-two years old after several failed dreams.

Don't let fear or failure stop you from answering the call.

Maybe you're thinking, *Okay, even if I do overcome fear, tell me this: How do I know when God is calling me?*

Let me begin my answer with a story.

Rich and I fell head over heels in love when we were seventeen, and we maintained a long-distance relationship from Miami, Florida, to Shreveport, Louisiana. We put in a lot of phone time, as you might guess. I will never forget when my mom came in with the first long-distance phone bill—that was a very real problem back then. When Rich would call our old-school landline, sometimes my brother Dez would answer. He was eleven at the time and sounded exactly like me. It was the joy of my brother's life to convince Rich that he was me. For a few moments, he would succeed, but sometime before the one-minute mark, Rich would figure it out and say, "Dez, put your sister on the phone!"

Dez couldn't fool him. Why? Because Rich knew me. He had spent countless hours talking to me. He knew the way I thought, the way I processed, the way I spoke—he knew *me*.

How do you hear the voice of God? Get to know him! Seek him and spend time with him. Read his Word and pray, and you will come to know his voice. Jesus invites you to be like sheep that trust their Good Shepherd, that "follow him, for they know his voice" (John 10:4). When you do, it will become a joy and life source for your soul, like it was for Job. He wrote, "I have treasured the words of his mouth more than my portion of food" (Job 23:12).

And when you sense him calling you into something new he is doing, honor him with your full attention and an open heart. When God revealed himself to Moses at the burning bush in Exodus 3, he told Moses, "Take off your shoes, this is holy ground." God was conveying to Moses, "This is not an ordinary moment. Awaken to the importance of this present place you stand." Give reverence when God is moving.

God is looking for men and women who recognize the urgency of that kind of moment, who won't delay in responding when he calls them. He is seeking those who will answer him like so many in Scripture did.

Abraham said, "Here I am" when God called him to leave his home country.

Jacob said, "Here I am" when God appeared to him in a dream.

Samuel said, "Here I am" as God called to him as a child in the temple.

Isaiah the prophet said, "Here I am" as God commissioned him to be a voice to the nations.

Ananias said, "Here I am" as God asked him to go pray for the Christian-killer known as Saul.

God seeks us individually with a once-in-history path that weaves together in the story he is telling.

He calls us to surrender with a heart that says, *I'm not running away or hiding; I'm worshiping. I won't cower in fear; I'll get lost in your love and move forward with your Spirit.*

The Deepest Reasons for Courage

When Moses heard God calling his name, he also answered, "Here I am" (Exodus 3:4). But after hearing God's big plans for him, Moses had questions: "Who am I that I should go to Pharaoh and bring the children of Israel out of Egypt?" (v. 11).

Moses was in a supernatural moment of purpose when suddenly the music stopped. *Who am I? Why me?*

"I will be with you," was God's answer.

"Who are you?" Moses asked next.

"I AM WHO I AM," God pronounced with authority (v. 14).

Perhaps you are thinking, *What in the world does that mean? That doesn't help clarify anything for Moses—or for me. I can't see how this could help me in my season of a slow burn.*

It's very important we take the time to discover what it means, because the two most important questions we will answer in life are: *Who am I?* and *Who are you, God?*

There is only one voice that can answer both of those questions—and it is the voice who spoke all of creation into existence.

He's the one who sent Moses to rescue the Israelites from slavery in Egypt, foreshadowing the greatest rescue mission that would happen years later.

Our Father God *saw* humanity in our misery. He *heard* our cries. Moved by his deep love, he sent his Son to rescue us.

And Jesus gave everything so we would know who God is and who we are in him.

Rick Warren put it this way: "It is only in God that we discover our origin, our identity, our meaning, our purpose, our significance, and our destiny. Every other path leads to a dead end."[3]

When have you found yourself in a "dead-end" place, at a loss about what makes you you, why you're here, and what you're made for?

We all have our own versions of this because it's hard to find clear answers in our world. Our culture is obsessed with identity. Everyone is searching for their sense of distinction and significance, processing every step publicly instead of letting transformation occur inwardly. People have never been prouder to declare who they are, yet we have never been more confused about our identity. There are many opinions but only one truth.

Our identity comes from knowing who God is. This is why, when Moses was questioning himself, God answered, "I will be with you."

Jesus fulfilled God's definitive statement, "I am who I am," when he made seven powerful "I am" statements during his time on earth.

I am the Bread of Life.
I am the Light of the world.
I am the Door.
I am the Good Shepherd.
I am the Resurrection and the Life.
I am the Way, the Truth, and the Life.
I am the True Vine.[4]

CALLING THE WARRIOR WITHIN

When you discover who Jesus truly is, you realize that his life, death, and resurrection are the bridge between these two questions we're exploring. You can't answer, *Who am I?* until you answer, *Who is he?*—because who he is changes who you are.

The message of Jesus says, "Because I died—not for you but as you—and because I came out of the tomb—not for you but as you—everything I have has now become yours."

And so, today, you can boldly declare:

I am forgiven.
I am justified.
I am a new creation.
I am healed by his wounds.
I am bone of his bone and flesh of his flesh.
I am resurrected to new life.
I am the light of the world.
I am a city set on a hill.
I am the salt of the earth.
I am a child of God.
I am an heir of God.
I am an imitator of God.
I am led by the Spirit of God.
I am saved by grace through faith.
I am kept in safety wherever I go.
I am strong in the Lord and in the power of his might.

In the slow burn, we often forget who we are.

Take a moment to consider: Have you forgotten who God says you are?

He says it again today. He calls you by name *again*.

Maybe you have ignored his call, running away and hiding—

but again he calls. It's not too late to answer and receive the strength you need to walk in your identity, to know in your bones that all he says about you is true.

You are not who God says you are only when you reach your goals, succeed in the eyes of others, or receive validation.

You are an overcomer and a conqueror *right now*.

Can You Say It Again?

My brother Lucas became a part of our family when he was a teenager. He had been a classmate of my brothers and ended up staying at our home over time due to some family difficulties. I have watched him mature into an incredible man of God, and I've seen our stories unite us, forming us into a family. The different colors of our skin remind me of how God binds people together and creates a true sense of belonging. We celebrated as Lucas graduated and became an honored local police officer who went on to bring so much good to our city. Today Lucas is truly a cultural change agent in his field.

When he got engaged several years ago, my dad told him, "Lucas, if you want to carry my last name, it's yours. No pressure, you are already my son; but if you desire to have it, it's yours."

The week of their wedding, Lucas and his wife, Bri, surprised us by telling us they had decided to take on our family name.

The night before the wedding, at the rehearsal dinner, Lucas was feeling the enormity of the coming moments. My parents came and hugged him before all the guests arrived. "You know how much we love you?" they said to him. "You know how incredible this next season of your life is and all that God has prepared?"

After a pause, he replied honestly, "Yes, but can you say it again?"

And before anyone else walked in, they surrounded him and spoke love and life to his heart.

"You're a great man, and you will be a great husband and father."

"You were born for this moment. It's your finest hour."

"The best is in front of you. You're covered and God is faithful."

These were truths for Lucas to hold in his heart, not only on his wedding day but in every moment that would follow. He needed reminding—we all do sometimes.

There are truths for you to hold on to as well. Do you need to hear the heart of our Father say it again today?

He came from heaven to earth to tell you, *I am with you.*

You have his name.

He has so much goodness ahead of you.

Listen to him.

I can see Moses leading the people out of slavery, facing the Red Sea, and saying to God, "I know you said it at the burning bush, but can you say it again?" And then God proclaiming, "I am with you!" before he split the Red Sea.

I can see Moses leading the people into the wilderness and discovering they had no food. "God, can you say it again?" And God sent manna from heaven to feed his people.

When Moses needed direction, maybe he repeated, "Can you say it again?" Then God sent the cloud by day and fire by night.

What if you and I did the same? In every season and in every step, we can ask God to tell us again and again who we are in him.

And that is the power of the wait. It leads us to see and know the one who is with us always. The one who doesn't turn away as we wait but stays close. The daily office of surrendering our lives to God every morning and night reminds us that he is with us, that he is our Source, and we want his plan.

A waiting season surrendered to God brings about more fruit than any mountaintop race in your own strength ever could.

> A WAITING SEASON SURRENDERED TO GOD BRINGS ABOUT MORE FRUIT THAN ANY MOUNTAINTOP RACE IN YOUR OWN STRENGTH EVER COULD.

Perhaps you are in a season where you need the loving voice of God to remind you of who you are and who he is. Maybe you are hiding, and you didn't even realize it. He's waiting.

Will you listen to him now? He has arranged this moment to speak his love over you again. When you remember who he is, you can remember who you are in him. And you won't have to hide; instead, you'll stand with freedom and strength, all because you are carrying the identity and love he has given you.

It all starts by simply saying, "Here I am."

CHAPTER 6

Deep in My Soul Instead

About ten years into marriage, Rich and I moved into a beautiful loft in the heart of Miami. This was before we had children, so we needed just a one-bedroom home. The view of the ocean from this place was incredible—that was the primary reason we rented it. The windows reached to the ceiling, and every morning I woke up inspired by the beauty of Miami.

That is, until a few months in, when I saw a sign go up for construction in the lot next to the water. A company would be building an apartment complex much bigger than our ten-story high-rise, one that would block our view of the ocean and pretty much everything else.

I was incensed. But we didn't own the loft, so I soon decided to let my frustration go, especially as I began watching how they would bring that mammoth to life. I had never seen anything like it, and I was intrigued to track the daily construction progress.

Workers showed up every morning for two years, faithfully preparing the land and building on it. I was surprised to see them spend months simply digging in dirt, plowing deeper and deeper into the earth. Nine months in, they poured concrete into the depths, and by the one-year mark, it still looked nothing like the renderings on the Coming Soon signs. There were no impressive results, so what was all the work about?

I couldn't follow it all exactly, but I saw them creating pipelines, evening the ground, and doing a myriad of other tedious-looking tasks with care. The workers kept at it daily while the site appeared completely the same for a *long* time. The foundation work took what felt like forever.

It was the perfect correlation for me that year as Rich and I were building our own foundations—establishing a new community of faith in Miami and continuing our faith journey of having a family.

Interestingly, once the building's foundation was built, the structure seemed to pop up overnight. After all that careful work, something new could start appearing before our eyes.

I wonder if there are foundations God is establishing in your life right now. What might they be?

Perhaps you can't wait for some kind of "building" in your life to begin when in fact it already has. You're looking to the heights, expecting a new structure to rise, not knowing it is time to establish a foundation in the depths. It is slow, tedious, calculated work, but everything that comes later depends on the quality of what is happening now.

Just think: No one ever comes to your home and praises the foundation; they never even see it. But it is the hidden strength of anything that is built to last.

I am teaching my four-year-old son to read right now; the process is tedious and not for the faint of heart. He often starts to read from right to left. Before I can move on to anything else, I need to establish that, in the English language, we read from left to right. He could know all his letters and sounds and even be a genius (of course, I think he is!)—but he will never be able to read if he skips this critical part. We cannot build any further until we lay the groundwork.

What is God establishing permanently in your heart in this season? How is he strengthening you in deep places and forming steadiness in you that you'll bring to every chapter ahead?

This Is What Our Creator God Does

Before we go any further, let me remind you that we're talking about *God* doing a work in your heart. It is something he *establishes*, and it's the kind of act he has been doing since the beginning of time.

The word *establish* means "to set up (an organization, system, or set of rules) on a firm or permanent basis,"[1] and we see it no less than 145 times in the Bible. In the Old Testament, God established a covenant of love with his people time and time again. In the New Testament, he established the new covenant of grace, the forgiveness of sins through Jesus' blood, and the hope of heaven. And God made it very clear in his Word that he and he alone established all of it:

> Who has ascended to heaven and come down?
>> Who has gathered the wind in his fists?
> Who has wrapped up the waters in a garment?
>> Who has *established* all the ends of the earth?
> What is his name, and what is his son's name?
>> Surely you know!
> Every word of God proves true;
>> he is a shield to those who take refuge in him.
>> (Proverbs 30:4–5)

> Yours is the day, yours also the night;
>> you have *established* the heavenly lights and the sun.
>> (Psalm 74:16)

> Your throne is *established* from of old;
> you are from everlasting. (Psalm 93:2)

When God established the mountains, he didn't ask anyone beforehand if it was okay. He is the Creator! He told the oceans where to lay their boundaries and the clouds what their pattern should be. He made them all exactly how he wanted them.

But when it came to humans, God gave free will. So the human heart is the only place where he yields. We need to open ourselves to him and welcome him to do his establishing work in us.

What might he do in you if you opened more of your heart to him?

Can you notice any areas where you might be holding back from him? Imagine how you could offer yourself more freely to your Creator God, who established the earth, the sun, your body, even your breath.

Remember that he wants to do this in you for your good! Jesus spoke about the importance of a strong foundation in Matthew 7:24–27, where he told the parable of the wise and foolish builders.

"Everyone who hears these words of mine and puts them into practice is like a wise man who built his house on the rock. The rain came down, the streams rose, and the winds blew and beat against that house; yet it did not fall, because it had its foundation on the rock. But everyone who hears these words of mine and does not put them into practice is like a foolish man who built his house on sand. The rain came down, the streams rose, and the winds blew and beat against that house, and it fell with a great crash." (NIV)

Storms come for us all.

The rain came down, the streams rose, and the winds blew

and beat against both the wise and foolish builders. Only one was rooted in Jesus, the only firm foundation.

Taking your child out of church during his preteen years for sports on Sundays appears fine when the sun is shining—but not when the wind begins to blow. Marrying someone who doesn't share your faith may seem okay until you need someone to agree with you in prayer when your child is ill. Having a peer group who is fun but doesn't have a foundation is easy until you need someone to encourage your soul in your darkest hour. You see what your foundation is made of—not what you say it is made of—when the weather in the wait takes a turn.

Designed to Stand Strong— and Get Stronger

The kind of foundation God will establish in you depends on where you are and what you're going to encounter.

In Miami we don't build for sunshine; we build for storms, and there is no better model for it than the palm tree. God designed them to be storm ready, deeply rooted, and built to last. Architects develop skyscrapers with the same approach as the palm—with a foundation built to allow the building to sway slightly as it withstands high winds. Many trees don't survive storms, but the palm was created to thrive.

As Psalm 92:12 says, "The righteous flourish like the palm tree and grow like a cedar in Lebanon." When the winds blow, the palm trees bend, but they don't break.

In the fall of 1992, Hurricane Andrew assaulted the foundation of Miami in a way like never before in history. Winds ripped through South Florida with a vengeance at 165 miles per hour, taking out everything in its path. Terrified and shocked, people watched as the storm flattened acres of land and ripped the strongest structures to shreds, ultimately leaving twenty-six billion dollars' worth of damage in its wake.[2]

Nothing could withstand the force of the wind and rain—except one thing.

The palm.

Which God had established.

Many of the leaves had fallen off and the bark had been cut away, but the roots—the foundation, if you will—remained unshaken.

Here is another extraordinary quality of palms: Storms actually make them *stronger*. They actually grow taller after each storm. And they produce fruit in every season.[3] The unpredictability of the tropics cannot tear it down or stifle its fruit. God established it to stand strong, to not only withstand storms but grow from them, and to bear fruit in every season.

If God will do that for the palm tree, how much more for the soul he loves?

You may be in the storm of your life today, with the wind raging and the rain falling, but what God has established in your life will not be moved.

Your identity is secure in Jesus. Your children will be pursued for all of their days by his perfect love. God is in your marriage with you, and a cord of three strands is not easily broken.[4] You will withstand the wind with an inner strength that only gets stronger as you wait out the weather.

God can establish you to be strong in every season of your life so that, when the storms of life come, they will only make you stronger, grow taller, and bear more fruit!

What should have destroyed you will grow you.

What should have defeated you will strengthen you.

Because you are established in him.

Building Roadways from Roots

If we want God to do establishing work in our hearts, how does it happen? What can we do to foster it?

Evangelist Anne Graham Lotz once said, "I read God's Word when I am not suffering. And then I don't have to all of a sudden establish this habit when I am hurting."[5] Spending time with God in Scripture and prayer is a way for us to actively invite God to form who we are at the deepest level. And that foundation, or those roots, will determine our reaction to life's challenges. You can make the choice to participate with God in nurturing a root that will serve you later.

A root is a commitment, and your commitments prepare you for crossroads—in your marriage, your purity, your language, your participation, your purpose. You decide now how you want to live in these areas, according to your values, so later, in the moment, you don't have to deliberate. It has already been established.

In your marriage: Establish your choice to speak life before you even get into that argument. Establish that divorce is not an option before you want to step out.

In your friendships: Establish that you don't gossip before you go on that lunch break with your coworkers.

In your job: Establish you will walk with integrity before the opportunity to cheat, embezzle, or lie comes around.

In your quiet time with God: Establish a daily pace.

In your generosity: Establish your generosity before the preacher gets up to share for the offering—settle it!

In your home: Establish that on Sundays you will go to church—do this before you wake up and you're sleepy on Sunday morning. If there's a baseball game, baby shower, holiday, birthday, or anniversary on a Sunday, we still find ourselves in the house of God. This doesn't have to be anxiously discussed or constantly brought up. Let your values establish your rhythm.

Every time we do these things, we are working with God to establish what is deep within us. Putting down roots means, "I'm putting my feet down." Scripture warns us not to be double-minded, leaving us to get tossed back and forth like the waves.[6] Crashing like waves, seeing the results of your energy fade back into the ocean, living aimlessly and chaotically—that is not God's plan for our lives. It may feel like a rush every now and then, but it's one step forward and two steps back.

Resolve to say, "I'm not a wave. I'm a palm tree. I choose where I'm planted. I have a singular source. Check me any day of the week."

God is looking for hearts that will put a stake in the ground, not come and go like waves. When others wander, we can say, "I'mma be here, by my Father's side. You go do your thing. But I'm not going anywhere. You won't have to look when you want to find me. I didn't go anywhere. I'm planted."

The roots we grow with God will create roadways to our future. We may see all the roads blocked in our lives in our season of waiting, but the real pathways of our life are found in our roots. And nothing circumstantial can ever stop their ever-expanding reach if your heart is surrendered. We always can dig deeper and grow stronger in him, which will keep guiding and enlivening us for all that is ahead.

In the Sacred, Secret Place

Let's come back to that key question: If we want God to do establishing work in our hearts, how does it happen? What can we do to foster it?

I'll tell you this: It is not through meticulously curating what is seen and temporary instead of what is unseen and eternal. We may share our devotional life with others—even present it beautifully on social media—but is it truly anchoring for our soul?

There are days I want to throw my phone into the ocean, never to see it again. My desire for this hit a peak in 2020, when we all were social distancing and there was so much chaos in the world. While I was glued to social media just like everyone else, I constantly longed for a deeper, truer experience in my soul—to not simply project peace but to dwell in peace.

Rich and I had started a nightly Instagram Live to encourage people; to this day I still hear reports from those who found real joy and hope through those candid conversations in our kitchen. I shared the recipes we used while staying at home, posted encouraging words, sang spontaneous duets a cappella with my brother Dee, shared my kids' daily routines, and even discussed marriage and renewed my vows online. It was fruitful and beautiful but also exhausting. What lasted for a season had a needed expiration date.

On my birthday that year I acknowledged in writing, for myself and for God, that rather than living my life on social media, I wanted to experience it "deep in my soul instead."

I didn't just write it; I meant it. I craved the deep end, the intimate, the sacred. I resisted the urge to post every beautiful moment and instead celebrated it in my heart, holding it close and relishing the intimacy of communion with God instead of with so many strangers. I felt a deeper knowing with him start to form as I valued tasting significant moments, not just capturing them.

The next month I received a package from a dear friend. Inside was a beautifully framed custom art print that simply read, *Deep in my soul instead.* It was like God was affirming the decision I had made to keep some sacred moments protected. I hung it in my bedroom and still see it every day; it reminds me of how I want to live and who I want to become with God. I'll choose to bring the "salted and pure and sacred" incense of my daily worship to my King, not the crowd, just like Aaron did in the tabernacle each day.

We love to try to curate reality. And that works great for the beginning of anything, but it's not something we can sustain. If we try to, we will sacrifice our peace on the altar of appearance. Roots are reality—not our appearance, not others' perception of us. If we try to make those things our source, our souls will starve. They don't have the capacity to be our strength.

We all have versions of this human experience of missing out on what we're made for. Do you know what your version is? Try to imagine how you could give more energy to your inner life with God, to experience more of the richness in the deep end, the intimate, the sacred. He is lovingly calling you to it.

After Mary's encounter with God, she "pondered . . . in her heart" the wonders he revealed (Luke 2:19, NIV). Some things you don't publish. Some things you don't present to the world to consume. Some things are too intimate to share and too sacred to speak of until you have his release.

In the meantime, know that he will build upon the sacred secrets within your soul. I have found that my roots now reach and yearn for his revelation, which revives my spirit and creates an intimate communion at the table of my heart. There is a deep joy that comes with living out Paul's words in Colossians: "As you received Christ Jesus the Lord, so walk in him, *rooted and built up in him* and *established* in the faith" (2:6–7).

Resilient at the Core

Eventually all the truth that has taken root deep within you will bear witness to the world. It is something you never could manufacture on your own; his Spirit miraculously accomplishes it in you in his time.

The resolve to protect and nurture the sacred intimacy you were made for requires patience. It is a private work, and it is not simply waiting. *Patience* is the ability to endure difficult circumstances, delays, or challenges without becoming frustrated or upset. It is accepting the challenge of the long haul with fervor and devotion, and it is the key to thriving in the slow burn of our life on earth.

James encouraged believers, "Be *patient* . . . until the coming of the Lord. See how the farmer waits for the precious fruit of the earth, being patient about it, until it receives the early and the late rains. You also, be patient. *Establish* your hearts, for the coming of the Lord is at hand" (5:7–8).

Patience requires continual care throughout the wait, but its power is life-changing. It creates a firm emotional foundation within you that will ultimately impact everything around you—often without even a word from you. It creates stability and perseverance.

Psalm 1 tells us that anyone who stays close with the Lord and delights in him is "like a tree planted by streams of water, which yields its fruit in season and whose leaf does not wither— whatever they do prospers" (v. 3 NIV). God's work in you undergirds everything that your life will build and establishes you in strength for every season.

It also brings you true *balance*—a word that can carry an empty meaning in our culture. It is not about having perfectly scheduled calendars or simply prioritizing self-care. I see God's picture of balance when I look at a tree. Its balance does not come from having perfectly symmetrical branches and leaves, all cut to mirror one another in equal weight and height. No, the branches vary in size, and the fruit at any given time is not putting equal weight distribution on each branch. The balance comes from the roots, the foundation, from what you don't see.

Further, if a tree's branches are perfectly cut to be pleasing and balanced to the eye but the tree is not rooted, it will fall over with the first gust of wind—because its balance doesn't come from the branches. It comes from the roots.[f]

We see another version of this in the way God designed our bodies. Our core—the stomach, lower back, pelvis, and hips—establishes our strength, just like the foundation of a building or the roots of a tree. I've heard it said that our core is like Wi-Fi; when it is strong, it connects everything in our body, and when it is weak, there are disconnections. With every step and stretch, in every moment of sitting or sprinting, our core is creating stability and a balance that sustains us. A resilient core prevents injury and prolongs health, but it takes time and dedication to strengthen.

The people of Okinawa, Japan, are known for having staggering longevity, and some of their daily movements are likely part of the reason why. Throughout each day, they sit on tatami mats on the floor; rising from the floor again and again requires flexibility and strength. This daily movement, as simple as it is, effectively contributes to their reputation of having one of the longest life expectancies in the world.[7]

How often we just want to focus on reaching high! But true strength comes when we are willing to return low again and again.

May we listen for God calling us back to the secret place so he can establish more and more strength in us for the slow burn.

---

f. See appendix for the handwritten journal entry.

Choosing the Confident Life in God

Dallas Willard observed, "We are becoming who we will be—forever."[8] He also noted, "The most important things in our human lives are nearly always things that are invisible."[9]

Where are you planted today? Or have you been living more of a "wave life" lately? Consider what your current choices are leading you to become.

Maybe you feel confused because you are ahead of God's process.

We cannot have the fruit without first growing the roots.

Perhaps you've been focusing more on what everyone can see and less on what is really going on within you.

You were made for the deep-end life, for sacred intimacy in the secret place with him.

It is a gift to be known by others—of course you need that in your life—but true transformation takes place in the heart. And God wants to create the core of your spiritual and emotional strength, which will support everything you will see built in the slow burn.

Whatever is visible to others will simply be the outworking of your inner state, and God will use that for his purposes. God has called us to establish his kingdom on earth, but the foundation of any external change is predicated by God first establishing our hearts.

Once you shift into this mindset, it will fill you with confidence. You can take courage in knowing that God is guiding you in wisdom and that all the work he does in you is *permanent*.

As a little girl, I gave my life to Jesus so many times. I cannot name a specific date when I first put my faith in him; I just know that, at some point, I finally started believing what he had already begun. I was established in him, but for so long I kept doubting—wondering if I had prayed passionately enough, wondering if he really heard me and changed my soul.

God wants you to walk in total confidence, knowing that your heart has been established by him and for him.

You don't have to try to get saved every Sunday like I did, or wonder if God has a plan for you, or question if you were meant to serve him. He has begun this work; now let him carry it out to completion. He will use the slow burn to establish you moment after moment. Heartbeat after heartbeat.

God's work of establishing your heart is no one-time event. Nor is it sporadic, with God clocking in and out, working only set hours. He doesn't abandon what he begins or move on to a bigger opportunity. Our God is too big and too faithful for that!

You are not a project to him; you are his masterpiece whom he loves. Everywhere you go, every moment of your life, he is establishing you. In every heartbeat that you are waiting, he is working and making his strength your strength.

All throughout the slow burn, let the Spirit of God search you and build in you, deep in your soul instead, knowing that the Architect is masterful.

And he always completes what he starts.

CHAPTER 7

Who's Waiting on Whom?

I have a friend who just barges in whenever he comes over to our house—no knock, no warning. Before I know we have company, he has already strolled in through the front door. He means well, but I laugh as I think of telling him, "Even Jesus knocks!"

On the other hand, I often get stuck outside the doors of our church offices because I've left my key at home. It has happened so often that the staff now knows the sound of my knock, the one I do as I stand outside with my arms full, just waiting for someone to hear me and let me in.

You know who also knows about standing at doors, waiting for them to open? Jesus. He once described his heart toward his people by saying, "Here I am! I stand at the door and knock. If anyone hears my voice and opens the door, I will come in and eat with that person, and they with me" (Revelation 3:20 NIV). These were words directed to the Laodicean church, but the spirit of his message applies to you and me today.

It is not a one-time welcome but a daily invitation to walk with him.

How do you allow God to establish your heart? You let him in.

He asks you for your surrender and cooperation. Even now, he stands at the door of your heart and wants you to know he is there waiting. How will you respond to him?

The promise for every person who hears his voice and opens the door is almost unthinkable: the indwelling of his very Spirit. The greatest miracle of the gospel is that we have a God who wants to live in our hearts!

When Ezekiel prophesied about this revolutionary work, he described God's incredible message to his people like this: "I'll give you a new heart, put a new spirit in you. I'll remove the stone heart from your body and replace it with a heart that's God-willed, not self-willed. I'll put my Spirit in you and make it possible for you to do what I tell you" (36:26–27 MSG).

God wants to establish all that you are moment by moment. And while there is plenty for you to wait on in this season, you don't have to wait to hear him speak to you. He's speaking now and waiting for you to listen.

It's important to get this picture, because it begs the question, *Who is waiting on whom?*

Again, Jesus is not inviting you to a one-time door swing of salvation here. In the original context in Revelation, Jesus was speaking not to the lost but to the found—to believers. He was revealing that the eternal life he has for us can be present for us now.

You know me and I know you. I'm knocking at your heart's door.
I want to have a conversation.
I want to come in and sit at the table with you.

Jesus wants to be with you. Every day. The God of the cosmos is pursuing you persistently. He is coming to you not just for salvation—though that would be enough for his broken creation—but also for relationship.

I think most of us assume that, if we have given our lives to

Jesus, we already have opened our heart to him. "Of course I want to please God. I want to know him. I welcome him in my heart." But when he knocks daily, what do we do?

Many times, it's a lot like the very first earthly response to Jesus' knocking.

Are We Listening?

Since the beginning of his journey to rescue humanity, Jesus has been knocking on doors. When his parents addressed the door of an inn, asking for space to give birth, the response was rejection. *No room.*

Instead of going back to heaven and giving up, the King of kings was born in a stable. The animals welcomed him more than the very people he came to save.

All the earth had been waiting for the Messiah and, after centuries of prophecies that he indeed would come, he transcended time and space and arrived at humanity's door. And he was greeted with, "Sorry, there's no room."

And, just like two thousand years ago, if the ears of my heart are not expectant and listening today, my response is the same. *Sorry, no room.*

I'm busy; I'm preoccupied.

I'm worried; I'm stressed.

My hands and my heart are way too crowded already.

Even in the waiting seasons of life, I can miss the Messiah I have prayed for even as he stands on my doorstep.

And yet he waits with a patience that only an eternal God can have.

My son Wyatt hasn't been able to hear very well for the past year and has failed multiple hearing tests. Soon he will have an ear surgery that our doctor said will change his life, and I cannot wait to see him enjoy the full functionality of that sense he has been missing.

Of course, I know that, even though he'll be able to hear perfectly, I still will spend the next ten years of my life saying what every parent says: "Listen to me." Being able to hear is not the same as choosing to listen and obey.

As Jesus said again and again, "Whoever has ears, let them hear" (Matthew 11:15 NIV).

I have received salvation, so I have been given the ability to hear. Today he is at the door of my heart knocking. Am I listening?

Today Jesus' words in Revelation 3:20 go out to our modern church, which has answered every invitation but the one that matters. It is an indictment of our preoccupation with our self-sufficiency. Some of us are so distracted with serving God that we cannot hear God. We have built high, but our foundation is weak. And it is all because, day after day, we have been telling him there is no room.

The irony of the human heart telling Jesus, "There is no room" is that the heart is simultaneously haunted by a void that leaves it always desiring more. How can there be no room and yet we also feel empty?

What is the *more* if not the Messiah?

All my kids love toys. What kid doesn't? My son Wilde is in a season of wanting new things constantly, and it's a daily conversation of gratitude for us. The other day he was talking about a supercool race-car toy he wanted—no, in fact *needed*—right now.

Feeling motherly, I quickly responded, "Wilde, you have already more toys than anyone could dream of."

With deep sincerity (which he seemed to actually believe), he pleaded, "I just want one more!"

How can I judge him when so often we hold the same blind perspective? C. S. Lewis once described human history as "the long terrible story of man trying to find something other than God which will make him happy."[1]

We feel like we are waiting for whatever the "more" is, when really Jesus is waiting on us. So I ask you, One more *what*? One more raise? One more recognition? One more great weekend, pair of shoes, or streaming service? We keep accumulating everything while holding nothing.

Jesus knocks in the morning and, with my phone pressed to my face, the answer without even a word is: *no room*.

Sometimes I literally miss a knock at our front door because our house is filled with noise. The same is true for the noise in my mind and in my life. Social media, endless to-dos, the constant replay of situations, work, family, celebrations, commitments—the list goes on.

At some point there has to be a choice to silence the noise. To say no to some things so we can say yes to him. We know from Psalm 46:10 that God is saying, "Be still, and know that I am God."

If we want to be in relationship with the one we were made for, we will need to value being still enough to hear his knock each morning and welcome him.

He's Coming to *In-habit*

Once we welcome him, what do we expect him to do? To simply stand at the door as it opens and quickly say a few kind words before he goes to the next door? Sometimes that's how we've treated him when he knocks. We'll say a short morning prayer and later throw out "see you later" before going to sleep.

But notice: Jesus is knocking to *come in*.

The question is not only whether you will hear the knocking and welcome him. It is also: Will you truly let him in? Let him see you, know you, and be with you as you are?

Is there room "in the *in*"—the deepest part of you?
    The interior? The intimate?
In the private pain of your life.
In the insecure narrative of your thoughts.
In the fears of *What if I fail again?*
In the secret sin.
In the chaos of your family.
In the instability of your emotions.
Will you let him in the *in*?

You may believe he can do miracles, but do you believe he can do miracles *in you*?

Perhaps you think your life is too messy. Remember, Jesus was born in a stable. From the beginning he has made it clear: *I'm coming for the mess! I didn't come to play church. I'm here for radical life change starting from the inside out. I am not coming just to make you look good; I'm coming to establish every heartbeat of your life with strength.*

And today he waits for you to welcome him in.

Here is the "so wild it's hard to believe" part: When you say yes to Jesus, when you say "there's room in the *in*," your heart is no longer the limit of your human experience. You find that your entire life is hidden in his heart. He tucks you in his wings, in the secret place, in the cleft of the rock. He hides you in his strength, his peace, his faithful arms. And your foundation becomes solid and secure, because you are allowing the Savior to sustain you.

The God of the universe desires to *in-habit* your life.

How often do we want him to change our life situation, yet we will not let him change our habitation? *God, I'm waiting on you—but don't dig too deep. I'm ready to build high.*

The truth is that he will tell us when we are ready to build high. First and foremost, we need to deeply internalize his Word and sustain a vibrant prayer life. We want our inner life to be defined by welcoming him in daily, listening and learning from him, and celebrating his presence and love.

The Joyous Meal That Never Ends

Conversations of substance are best held while sitting. For small talk, we stand. For real conversations, we find some chairs. Ideally a table with a beverage and a bite. This is what Jesus is after when he knocks at our door. He wants to walk in and sit at the table of our heart.

"I will come in and eat with that person, and they with me," he said (Revelation 3:20 NIV).

This is the opposite of Uber Eats—which I love. I've ordered birthday cakes, sushi, baby formula, and of course a million pizzas. The options, the speed, and the convenience—how can I resist?

Apparently, I am not alone. The North American fast-food industry is set to break $300 billion in revenue, and projections are only rising.[2] The quick rise to global domination is understandable. We love choices, fast and easy. We get what we like, when we want it, wherever we want it. It perfectly reflects our modern mindset.

Jesus is the Bread of Life, but he is not Uber Eats. We don't simply tip him for the saving grace he provides. He isn't dropping it near the door and heading out to the next stop. He *is* the door—the fulfillment you're looking for. He isn't just fast food; he's the foundation of all.

To understand the experience at the table Jesus wants to have with us, we must grasp the vast differences between ancient and modern food cultures. The society of Jesus' time highly valued communal meals. It wasn't an individual experience where you order what you want and eat in your car on the way to the next thing. It was an experience that involved preparation and rituals, and it was centered around not simply eating but on sharing and spending quality time together.

In our big Louisiana family, there are many nights around the table we don't want to end. We sit together until we can barely keep our tired eyes open, putting our farewells off as long as we can, but at some point, everyone must go home.

But with Jesus, it doesn't have to end. He is the friend who sticks closer than a brother. He sings over us as we sleep. He wakes us with new mercies. He sits at the table of our hearts again and again and, before we know it, things begin changing from the inside out.

I often have felt overwhelmed by the command in Scripture to "pray without ceasing" (1 Thessalonians 5:17). It is perplexing to attempt to always talk to someone. But I have come to believe that the encouragement to pray without ceasing is based on the promise of an ever-present God.

The wonder and work of the wait is found in reveling in the presence of the Creator of the universe at the table of your heart. It's a wonder for us that Jesus stays "without ceasing." His great mercy never ceases. His steadfast love never ceases. His limitless power never ceases. We pray without ceasing because *why would we not* talk to the one who never ceases to be *in* our most inner struggles and dreams.

At any given moment we can say, *Jesus, you're here with me.*

You don't come to me only when I'm achieving or pressing on.
You're closest when I'm broken, and you love me.

One of my favorite names of God is Emmanuel. God with us. He is with us. Are we with him?

How often do I sit at tables entertaining others, not realizing that Jesus sits at the table waiting for me? How often do I usher him out of the war room of my heart while I struggle on the mountains I face alone? How often do we make plans as if we are the architects of our future without even a nod to the one who made the blueprint of our life before we took our first breath?

What of the slow-burn nature of our God? He is "merciful and gracious, slow to anger, and abounding in steadfast love and faithfulness" (Exodus 34:6). I, too, can say like Paul "that in me, as the foremost, Jesus Christ might display his perfect patience as an example to those who were to believe in him for eternal life" (1 Timothy 1:16). He doesn't walk in only to violently flip the table of my heart without a word. He sits with me and dines with me, and as we commune together, the tables start to miraculously turn.

Who Else Is at the Table?

As Jesus sits down, he sets a table before us, sometimes in the presence of our enemies.[3] Sometimes we are entertaining enemies of our heart without even knowing it—yet he still stays close. The more we listen to his voice, the more we see the truth and the need for some of our guests to leave.

There are some characters sitting at your table right now that are complicating your conversations with Jesus. In time, you'll likely show the door to those imposters.

Perhaps you have invited Fear to your table. I know what it's like for fear to complicate my conversations with God. There's nothing as paralyzing as fear. As I have welcomed Jesus to my heart's table time and time again, I know that his "perfect love casts out fear" (1 John 4:18). *See ya.*

Have you welcomed Regret into your wait? Counseling can be such a help; it has been good for me. But even with the right support, it's hard to get rid of regret, and it can severely limit you. *Regret* is the person who is so conscientious that they rarely slip up—and when they do, they cannot let it go. They focus only on the strikeouts, never the wins.

What about welcoming Pride? Relying on our own strength and what others think of us weakens you deeply. Today you can place an eviction notice, because there's a new guest at the head of the table.

Another beautiful part of having Jesus at the table of your heart daily is that new companions start to join you. Wisdom, Understanding, and Discernment are new guests. And the soul food starts to look different. Perhaps you have been feasting on gossip, drama, self-loathing, or perfectionism—if so, you know it eventually makes you feel sick. But now you can feast on *love, joy, peace, patience, kindness, goodness, gentleness,* and *self-control.* You can feel healthy and revived. And it's all because you let him in! The foundation starts to transform, and our strength is suddenly not our own.

It all starts with listening for his knocks and welcoming him in.

And know that sometimes he will knock at the most unexpected moments and in the most unexpected ways.

One night after a long day at work, I sprinted into the house, trying desperately to get everything in shape before hosting friends and family. As I furiously scrubbed the dishes at the sink, attempting to set a world record for speed, I felt a whisper in my heart. I had a strong thought impressed on me. *Can I wash your heart?*

My rush came to a full stop.

I stood silently at the faucet as the warm water continued to run over my hands. I realized that the dishes were not the most important thing that needed washing at that moment. I needed a heart cleanse.

As I took inventory within, I knew there was a lot of junk subtly stockpiled in my soul. Life had been full, and I was attempting to control the chaos by organizing the exterior. It had been a season of heart wounds, disappointing friendships, and sacrifice. Bitterness was getting cozy at my table. Judgment was trying to take a seat. And I had started to accept and believe I was entitled to keep their company.

My heart simply needed Jesus' habitation.

I finally had the ears to hear the knock I had been ignoring.

I turned off the faucet and opened the door of my heart. A loving, faithful, and patient God met me in my little kitchen that night and filled me once again with his abounding peace, forgiveness, and strength.

I wonder if you can be honest about what is going on in your heart today. Is there anything you might be withholding from the light, hiding away in another room of your heart?

Here is a truth that has taken me a long time to learn but has helped me be more honest with Jesus: That thing you can't talk about owns you. What is unseen is much more important than what is seen. The hidden parts of your heart are influencing every area of your life.

And Jesus wants to talk with you about it.

Knock, knock.

The moment is now.

Open the door like only you can.

Let him come in and be with you, exactly as you are in this moment.

CHAPTER 8

Connect the Dots

Fear is a chameleon, rearing its head in different colors depending on the season. It matches the tone of your thoughts and cunningly distorts your vision. It tells you to keep secrets from people you love just to save face, which isolates you in weakness. Left to keep trying to maintain your own individual, finite fortress, you eventually discover it will never lead you to true strength.

I know because I've lived it.

When I was twenty-five and my doctor referred me to an infertility specialist, I told my husband and no one else—and asked him not to share it with anyone. I did not want to become known for having this struggle. I was going to fix this problem before anyone even knew there was a problem. I would bring everyone in on it when I was on the other side of it, when it was a celebration, not a prayer request.

I never would have dreamed the journey would stretch out to eight years.

I went to the doctors' appointments alone. I had the procedures, managed my calendar, and showed up for work, all the while hoping I could fix the problem. But I couldn't. And it took me a full year to share with my parents. They were the safest place I could turn to, yet I avoided opening up to them. Why?

I must pause and think deeply as I reflect.

It's not as if we were not in touch; we spoke every day. And it's not that I expected my parents, who are my greatest champions and prayer warriors, to be unkind or awkward about it. I had no doubt they would speak only life and never judge. The secrecy had nothing to do with their character and everything to do with my own personal battle and lack of desire to "go there." In my head, "going there" would be heavy, emotional, and awkwardly raw. If only I had known it would lift a weight, bolster my faith, and surround me with safety.

I was buying the lie of isolation, believing my daily battle was only my own—even when it became obvious that I didn't have the strength to bear the weight of the journey by myself.

Still, I knew talking to my parents would make me feel exposed, and I was afraid of feeling that. I also didn't know how to face the complex mix of difficult emotions I had buried deep down.

Who isn't afraid of feeling exposed? We all have had excruciating moments we want to avoid ever repeating—so we self-protect by isolating. It's something we are especially tempted to do while we wait. We retreat to a safe place within ourselves, "just until the season has passed." I have not only done this myself but also witnessed it in others throughout the decades of working in our community.

You start the divorce process, and you disappear from community because it's easier in the present not to talk about it.

You lose your job and you back away from community because you feel embarrassed.

You step into a relationship, and you know your mentors will see red flags and you suddenly are too busy to meet up, all the while convincing yourself that they are the ones who changed.

Your peers start to get married and you feel like the odd one out, so you stop hanging with the friends you have walked with for years.

Why is everyone else moving so quickly into their hopes and dreams? you wonder as you curse your slow burn. Fireworks are going off all around you, and you're the dud. Instead of confronting how you feel, you isolate and hope it will pass.

And as you go on hoping the issue will pass, it is actually life that is passing you by.

What If You Unlocked the Door?

We all struggle with this not only because it is human nature, but because the Enemy is attacking us. If he can't get us paralyzed by fear, he will put on a new mask and convince us to pull away from our community of support and accountability—and that is when we are most vulnerable to his lies. When we are alone, his voice is the loudest.

No one can do the journey of life alone. We were created to do life together. A baby cries until he is held. Solitary confinement is considered torture. You also can be in a room full of people and still feel alone because loneliness has more to do with what's going on inside you than what is going on around you. So even if you are not physically isolated, a deep ache within persists.

When you are walking through a painful, vulnerable season, you might feel that you don't have the energy to "go there" with the people you love. The exposure feels so scary, and the emotions you have pushed down deep frighten even you.

But what do you think would happen if you unlocked the door to your inner life to those who know you the best?

I discovered the answer to this question a year into trying to start a family as I sat on a couch with my parents and shared the journey I had been on. The numerous procedures I had done without telling them and how they all were failures. How profoundly heartbroken and frustrated I was that, five years into marriage, we were nowhere near being able to start a family.

My parents held me in their arms, and then they kindly reminded me, "DawnCheré, this is not about you. You don't have to put the pressure on yourself. This is about an eternal soul coming into the world. At the right time, God will do it. You can trust him."

How does a hopeless journey suddenly re-shift into a completely different landscape in just a moment? Connection brings clarity and a bigger picture.

My story is God's story, and he has an eternal plan. This is not a toy doll I'm trying to acquire at the store; this is an eternal soul, destined for a particular time in history. May God's will be done.

God, I trust there is a bigger story at play. When I look at the grandness of your design, I can trust the story you are telling.

I could not get to that mindset on my own—because I am a human who needs other humans. And so are you. This mirrors the poetic words of Desmond Tutu: "My humanity is bound up in yours, for we can only be human together."[1] It also is a picture of why the book of Proverbs urges us to seek the wisdom of counselors. God steers us toward one another because he wired us to rely on one another. If we can only be brave enough to be honest with our safest people, we'll be positioned to receive the care and insight we so desperately need.

Guard the Life You Were Made For

"Be sober-minded; be watchful," Paul taught believers. "Your adversary the devil prowls around like a roaring lion, seeking someone to devour" (1 Peter 5:8). How does a lion destroy its prey?

By isolating them. He gets one all alone, without any protection, then ruthlessly attacks. A disturbing parallel is that 85 percent of violent crimes in America happen to people who are alone.[2]

Isolation changes our physical and psychological states; we release more stress hormones, our daily challenges feel more intense, and we are more prone to negative expectations. Again, God made us for more. The Enemy wants you to isolate yourself because he knows you were created to be connected.

So be on guard, God tells us. Be watchful in the wait.

When you isolate, you become the center of your world, and your desires become your entire focus. Eventually your life revolves around them. But nothing in creation was created to stand at the center all alone. Not even the Trinity operates this way.

Tim Keller described this in a compelling way in *The Reason for God*. I invite you to slowly soak in each word as it beautifully depicts what God invites us into.

> We will do things and give affection to others, as long as it helps us meet our personal goals and fulfills us.
>
> The inner life of the triune God, however, is utterly different. The life of the Trinity is characterized not by self-centeredness but by mutually self-giving love. When we delight and serve someone else, we enter a dynamic orbit around him or her, we center on the interests and desires of the other. That creates a dance, particularly if there are three persons, each of whom moves around the other two. So it is, the Bible tells us. Each of the divine persons centers upon the others. None demands that the others revolve around him. Each voluntarily circles the other two, pouring love, delight, and adoration into them. Each person of the Trinity loves, adores, defers to, and rejoices in the others. That creates a dynamic, pulsating dance of joy and love.[3]

This is what we were made for.

Is it any wonder isolation brings deterioration and connectedness brings life?

The Interconnectedness of Creation

Isolation is destructive because God has designed all of creation to be profoundly interconnected. We are more connected than we could ever dream—to an extent we won't even know till heaven. But the wise will pay attention to it here on earth.

It often begins with simply seeking and seeing what God is doing.

When was the last time you saw it?

Take a moment to look for it now. Open your eyes to the world around you. Take a step outside and breathe in the fresh air. All of creation is a supernaturally synced synergy of individual components that are inextricably linked. The individual exists to be connected to the whole. And we get to spend the slow burn of our entire life discovering all the connections he has made without our even knowing!

My husband's parents slept in the same travel crib as infants while living in two different states in the 1950s. It was passed to their parents from the same traveling evangelist who visited both of their towns. How they met decades later and married is only the providence of God and the delight of the connected path he creates for those who trust him.

Rich and I stayed at the same hotel for the same event one weekend when we were teenagers. We didn't meet until a year later in a different state. We were breathing the same air and walking the same halls completely unaware!

A friend recently shared that she went to the same preschool as her husband when they were three years old—but they didn't realize it for years. They are grandparents now, faithfully married all this time, and only recently connected the dots through an old picture one of them found. They had no idea the layers of what God was doing decades before they met.

There are roughly thirty trillion human cells in our body—think about connecting all those dots. The organs, limbs, muscle tissue, and countless other components of the body are all interconnected in a way only God could orchestrate.

When it comes to relationships, the historical concept of "six degrees of separation" has rapidly evolved to *three* degrees of separation with the advancement of technology and social media. Yes, you are three people away relationally to anyone else on the planet.[4] You are not isolated!

We have looked within and around, but what about up? Billions of stars in different galaxies are orbiting as the gravitational pull keeps them in orbit. Every star is a slow burn with nuclear fusion releasing light and heat; some of them hold enough energy to last hundreds of billions of years.[5] The stars closest to earth today had to have been burning over four years ago for us to see them right now.[6]

Astronomers can "look back in time" by studying those visible stars, since they are technically seeing them in their past. Talk about a slow burn of patience and perseverance. The ember of each star stands alone but reaches out across the dark expanse, offering direction to humanity throughout history. It is only through connecting the dots that we can see Orion, Ursa Major, Aquila, Lynx, and every other majestic constellation.

In *The Voyage of the Dawn Treader*, C. S. Lewis illustrated the deeper spiritual connection we share with all of creation. When one character said, "In our world . . . a star is a huge ball of flaming gas," a foreigner from another realm replied, "Even in your world,

my son, that is not what a star is but only what it is made of."[7]
If you simply look at the elements of earth and sky, you'll miss
the endless connections to the Creator. There are connections all
around you.

After you look up, within, and around, why not look down?
The dark sky above reminds me of the soil below. Seeds, packed
with hidden potential, settle into fertile soil and develop roots
deep below the earth's surface. Did you know there are more than
fifty thousand different types of seeds? At any given moment they
are beneath our feet, growing and stretching outward, forming a
network of touchpoints of creation.

Above us in the sky . . . *connect the dots.*
Within us in our bodies . . . *connect
   the dots.*
Below us in the soil . . . *connect the dots.*

May our wonder always outweigh our
knowing, because there are endless layers
to every dot and depth behind every connection. Could we spend all of eternity
connecting the dots of his glory?

MAY OUR WONDER ALWAYS OUTWEIGH OUR KNOWING, BECAUSE THERE ARE ENDLESS LAYERS TO EVERY DOT AND DEPTH BEHIND EVERY CONNECTION.

All of Our Stories Weave into His Story

My friend Melinda recently told me, "The only time I was invited
to church, I went. And my entire life changed as a result."

Rich and I were the ones who invited her—years ago, back
when we'd just started our local church gathering. We passed a
young mom pushing a stroller on the sidewalk, stopped and chat-
ted, then encouraged her to join us that Sunday.

She showed up. And she gave her life to Jesus, recommitting to a faith she had not held since her youth.

Committing to a small group of women gave Melinda a place of belonging, where people pray and support one another through tough seasons. Discipleship classes deepened her faith. Arriving early each Sunday, even with her three young boys in tow, gave her the chance to connect with other leaders and serve God's house.

Today Melinda is the longest-running team leader in our church after serving faithfully for almost a decade. Although she's had every reason to step away and lean into other things that need her time, she hasn't—because she found everything her heart had been searching for through community. Her children are now growing in their identity as sons of God, leaders at a young age, maturing before our eyes.

Melinda has become a part of the very net that was cast to capture her heart.

That's a single dot suddenly and forever connected to an eternal family. A soul wrapped up in love and brought into the fold of the body of Christ, where we unify the isolated and encourage the disheartened.

So often we measure ourselves alone, unaware that our strength is in unity. We don't realize where our fulfillment comes from because we're isolated in a story that was created to be infinitely intertwined. Every dot of history is connected in his story.

I grew up spending time in my parents' music studio, singing their original music. One ordinary day after school, I wrote my first song, entitled "The One Who Waits." (I know, I know—how many songs about waiting are part of this story? Only God could have orchestrated it all!) I recorded the song in Nashville on my first album, the lyrics of a longing heart set to R&B and pop vibes. I hadn't met Rich yet, but I was already waiting for the love of my life.

Somewhere out in the world there's someone thinking of me.
He doesn't know my name but I'm his destiny.
Here I am waiting for someone who'll fill up my dreams.
Keeping myself for him, knowing he'll come to me.

I don't know where he is, I don't know when he'll be mine.
It may not be today, but he'll be right on time.
Will it be his smile or the look in his eyes?
Will our love slowly grow or take me by surprise?

I believe I'm on my way, growing closer every day,
to the moment when I'll see the one who waits for me.
When I see him I'll realize, all my waiting was worth the while.
He'll be more than I could ever dream, the one who waits for me.

I waited all through middle and high school, never going on a date until my senior year. Yes, we were babies when we met at seventeen—but I spent years making choices based on faith that something orchestrated by God was around the corner as I waited.

The waiting was definitely "worth the while." And our love totally took me "by surprise."

I met Rich in Nashville when I was recording music and he was visiting his brother, who was a friend of mine. We went to a concert with mutual friends, then went thrifting. Classic '90s move. When we parted ways that first night, Rich said, "I'll call you."

The next night we talked for hours on the phone. He told me about the radical change he'd experienced the month before when he'd felt called to ministry. In only a few weeks, he'd completely changed his life. His Jesus story was compelling and beautiful and naturally flowed out in that early conversation.

Before we hung up, he said, "Ask your parents if they know mine. I think they go way back."

To my amazement, I found out our families had been friends before my dad even met my mom. My parents had supported his parents when Rich's little brother had a severe health crisis.

Another one of Rich's relatives had mentored my mom when she was eighteen years old, then introduced my parents to each other a decade later.

David Wilkerson, Rich's dad's cousin, had been my father's greatest mentor and put food on our table for years as my dad preached monthly at Times Square Church.

Yet another of his relatives had sung at my parents' wedding and been their dearest friend.

How could all of this have been true? None of our family members set us up or even introduced us! And yet the very fabric of our lives was so deeply connected. And while I'd been waiting, Rich had been waiting on me to strengthen his decision to follow Jesus and walk alongside him for the journey ahead.

I tell you all of this to illustrate yet another connection in the story God is telling. "The One Who Waits" wasn't just the first song I wrote; it was a reminder to my heart that all my waiting is worth the while when God is the storyteller.

ALL MY WAITING IS WORTH THE WHILE WHEN GOD IS THE STORYTELLER.

Rest assured that God is weaving each of our individual stories into a tapestry that tells his epic story.

Zoom In, Zoom Out

In Miami we have the gift of enjoying the seashore with its stunning sunsets, glistening waves, and golden sand. Astronomers have long deliberated whether there is more sand on the seashore or stars in the universe. Connect enough dots of sand, a *lot* of them—roughly one billion grains of sand per cubic meter—and you have a shore.

United as one.

Just as the body of Christ is.

You are part of "the shore"; you aren't meant to function as a single grain of sand.

Unifying with God's story is a choice. When you look around you, do you see only disconnection, or the opportunity to connect? The difference between *random* and *destined* is your perspective.

Do you see yourself as a single dot, or as part of a divine galaxy?

Your view affects the way you treat the restaurant server, the insurance agent, the nurse—you never know what part they may play in your future or what part God desires you to play in theirs! Entertaining angels will make your every day alive with awe and wonder.

Being intentional about what you dwell on can do the same.

Every time I fly home to Miami, there is a point when all I can see out one side of the plane is the uninhabitable, swampy Everglades. But when I look out the other side, the landscape is bursting with signs of life—I know there are millions of people buzzing in a metropolis of culture and community. Both areas are available for me to focus on. How tragic would it be if somehow I could see only the swamps when so much vitality and connection is within my reach in the other direction?

Sometimes you just need to zoom out and see how much more is within reach.

Bring some other people into your lens. Take stock of your entire life story and rehearse all the ways God has delighted you and loved you. It's never too late to look out the window on the other side.

Keep in mind that one season doesn't define you, whether it is good or bad. When it's good, connect the dots: God gives favor. When it's bad, connect the dots: God is faithful. When it seems to be a wasteland, don't be surprised if God has more than you could imagine around the corner. What looks like disaster in the moment is often his providence.

When was the last time you took a long look at what God has done for you? Connect the dots and then tell someone about it. As you express what God is doing, it will fill your heart with awe and wonder.

And what about those days when, try as you might, you cannot seem to glimpse a broader view of the story? There is room for goodness there too—a way of meeting with God by "zooming in."

Often, to keep my kids quiet in church, I have them trace letters that I make with dots that connect. At times they get impatient waiting for me to draw each dot; it's a slow burn that could drive any preschooler crazy. There is a big difference between coloring in a shape that already has firm lines and starting with only dots that you have to connect. It takes longer to connect dots.

Sometimes God gives us a blueprint and other times he creates it dot by dot. When that's the case, we have to wait for him to create a point A that will connect to a point B—and then a point C. While we don't know how he's working, we do know our role: to fully trust and wait on him.

A lot of people reach for the coloring book instead of reaching for the Creator. It's faster to reach for a pattern than a unique purpose. Is the point to see the entire landscape of your life now or to know where he has you in this moment? Sometimes when we can't see the full picture, we just need to delight in today.

Walk with Your Eternal Family Now

The first year of trying to start a family, I just wanted to get to the prize. *Forget all the heart stuff, let's get a result. If I can just have a baby* . . . But I didn't realize that the season of waiting was about so much more than getting what I wanted.

I'd like to close this chapter by speaking to your heart a message I would speak to the younger version of myself if I could.

God has woven you into the interconnectedness of his creation and his story. You are not isolated and alone. Every part of you was created to walk in supernatural synergy with God, the world he created, and the people around you.

Cells separated are not a body. Stars separated are not a constellation. Sand separated is not a shore. People separated are not a community. And the slow burn separated from other embers is not an eternal fire. From the seashore to the galaxies and from bustling streets to open fields, he's always been telling his story through the unity of his people.

The work in your wait is to refuse to isolate.

THE WORK IN YOUR WAIT IS TO REFUSE TO ISOLATE.

You are heading to a heaven full of your eternal family and your God, who writes the best stories. He's leading you to that home now throughout this long slow burn on earth. Let the wait enlarge your vision of the way forward and help you follow him. Let it help you to see the dots he has put before you and to connect them.

When you do, you will silence the lies of the Enemy and not walk alone in cynicism but with a community in strength. You will sense more of what God is doing and how you are part of it through unity, seeing a bigger picture you never would have seen alone.

The day before I married my husband, my dad reminded me that you can't control where the bus of life goes, but you can control who is on your bus. You need people to laugh, suffer, and celebrate with in the wait. You need the slow-burn society.

Now is the time to stop trying to fight your battles alone. When you separate, you weaken the wait. I know you feel protected in your silo, but you are exposed there. Go get accountability and strength from a family of faith. Choose to stay connected.

Relationships don't just happen, and they don't stay strong without investment. It takes work to stay connected. Expect the effort.

Find someone who loves you and share what is really going on. Pick up the phone, make the coffee date, and open your mouth! Tell them about your wait and pain, and receive the care and strength their presence will bring. You were created to be connected all throughout the slow burn.

CHAPTER 9

Fan Flames in the Wilderness

E very Fourth of July growing up in Louisiana, fireworks were the main event. I couldn't resist going out with my crazy brothers and loading the car with every kind of pyrotechnic we could get our hands on.

The scariest thing in the world was to light a firecracker, back away, wait for it to pop, and then wonder, *Is it still lit?* I'd tiptoe up and look closer to see if it was. Sure enough, I'd catch a glimpse of the tiny spark—then run away quickly in case it was close to exploding.

Even if the flame was small, it was burning. There was indeed some power at work there.

Have you ever wondered if your faith was still ignited?

Asking that question is a vastly different kind of experience than checking a firework flame. It's not, *Is that thing going to explode into something awesome?* It's, *Do I have what it takes to keep going?*

We can see this kind of weariness and distress in David's words: "My days vanish like smoke; my bones burn like glowing embers" (Psalm 102:3 NIV).

We see it in many of the suffering people who crossed
    Jesus' path too.
The woman taken for adultery, exposed and
    vulnerable.
The leper, untouchable and virtually invisible.
The demon-possessed man, tormented by darkness
    and self-harm.
The paralytic, unable to move and function in society.
The woman with the alabaster jar, known for and
    judged by her past.
The thief on the cross, only breaths away from his
    death.[1]

There are other times we wonder whether our faith is still
ignited because we're stuck in a struggle. It seems like there's no
way to escape it and move forward.

I've had a number of seasons when I felt stuck in a desperate desire to revert back to a previous version of myself—one I
considered to be happier, steadier, and healthier. I felt this after
I became a mother and was trying to get the rhythm of my life
back. I felt it after a house move. I felt it as we continued to
expand our church family, navigating friendships, planting
new locations, and building our team. I'd tell myself to get it
together as I kept striving to get back to this "better" version I'd
been before.

What might your version of this be? Think of when you've
been able to relate to the words of U2: "You got stuck in a
moment, and you can't get out of it."[2]

How do you get out of a stuck place?

What do you do when your slow burn feels like a lot of smoke
and hardly any light?

Finding More Fire

Scripture points us to several things: Surrender to God as your source. Listen to the Spirit and align your will with his. And fan the flame of your faith by focusing on what God has revealed.

FAN THE FLAME OF YOUR FAITH BY FOCUSING ON WHAT GOD HAS REVEALED.

SURRENDER TO GOD AS YOUR SOURCE

A wick positioned in an oil lamp needs fuel, air, and stability to stay fully lit. When it doesn't have enough of those things, it becomes fragile. The smoldering wick can be smothered or snuffed out if it's not encouraged and protected.

We are like that smoldering wick when our perspective gets darker, our soul languishes, and our hope dwindles. Distraction, worry, and fear threaten to snuff out our faith as it smolders.

But Isaiah prophesied of a Savior coming to people like you and me who languish: "A bruised reed he will not break, and a smoldering wick he will not snuff out" (42:3, NIV).

Maybe you feel unsure if you have what it takes to persist in this season. Or you might fear your purpose is slipping away or that your potential will never be realized. Hold on to this truth: Jesus didn't come to disqualify you or condemn you. He came to be your source, just as he was for the leper, for the thief on the cross—for all the suffering people who crossed his path listed earlier in this chapter.

He wants you to depend on him and yield to him.

So fully surrender the pieces of your life to the Spirit of God and embrace the wait. Let his flame strengthen you from within. The light of his love casts out all fear. Your slow burn will not be quenched. And you will come to know the truth in Henri

Nouwen's words: "Our glory is hidden in our pain, if we allow God to bring the gift of himself in our experience of it."[3]

LISTEN TO THE SPIRIT TO ALIGN WITH HIS WILL

When I most recently felt stuck in the struggle of trying to be my former self, I eventually sensed the Holy Spirit renewing my mind and giving me a different perspective. I realized that, as I desired to go back, I was wielding my own strength for change and assuming I knew what was "right" for that season.

Meanwhile, God didn't want me to go back. He wanted me to transform into who he was calling me to be now, not yesterday, and that wouldn't happen if I was seeking a template I already knew. It'd come only from totally surrendering to him and seeking his will. *Not my will but yours, Lord.*

In the kingdom of God, there are no duplicates. No duplicate seasons, no repeats for every blade of grass, no copies of shells on the seashore. There is a living source of all creativity that is never ending, just waiting to lead and direct our lives if we would wait and listen.

In that moment of reflection, the promise came to life. Though I'd read it a million times, it felt brand-new: "His mercies are new every morning" (Lamentations 3:22–23). The mercies of yesterday had expired and would leave me stuck. I'd need what his Spirit held for today.

The catch here is that it takes total trust, because you're looking at a brand-new page with him. The unknown.

This is why it's easier to choose "will worship"—wielding our own will—instead of choosing the willingness to surrender. We like the path we know, the one our minds can grasp and our abilities can handle. And we get stuck, like I did.

We step into God's will by bringing him our wholehearted willingness to align with him, not insisting on "will worship."

Elisabeth Elliot described this path well when she said, "Waiting on God requires the willingness to bear uncertainty, to carry within oneself the unanswered question, lifting the heart to God about it whenever it intrudes upon one's thoughts."[4]

We cannot will our way out of a wilderness season. We can only bring fresh surrender to the altar and wait on the Lord.

> WE CANNOT WILL OUR WAY OUT OF A WILDERNESS SEASON. WE CAN ONLY BRING FRESH SURRENDER TO THE ALTAR AND WAIT ON THE LORD.

Fan Your Faith into Flame

It seems there was a time when Timothy questioned whether the flame of his faith was burning. Paul responded with certainty that it was indeed alight and guided him in nurturing it. He wrote,

> I am reminded of your sincere faith, a faith that dwelt first in your grandmother Lois and your mother Eunice and now, I am sure, dwells in you as well. For this reason I remind you to fan into flame the gift of God, which is in you through the laying on of my hands, for God gave us a spirit not of fear but of power and love and self-control. (2 Timothy 1:5–7)

Paul referred to Timothy's faith as a gift and urged him to *fan it into flame*.

Notice that it's not our job to light the flame of faith—that's the gift of God. Our job is to stimulate and energize our faith. To revive it when it seems to be subsiding. To encourage the power in it to rise and expand.

When the Israelites were in a stuck place, they did the *opposite* of this.

As their journey through the wilderness seemed never-ending, the group morale plummeted. They snowballed from discouraged to dissatisfied and from grumbling to catastrophizing. At one point they even wailed, "If only we had died in Egypt! Or in this wilderness!" (Numbers 14:2 NIV).

They'd forgotten all that God had done—the deliverance from Egypt, the miraculous march through the Red Sea, the destruction of their enemies.

In the moments they felt low, they had a choice: They could look back at what God had revealed about himself and put their trust in his faithfulness. Or they could focus on what they lacked in the present and give up waiting for the total fulfillment of the promise.

And they went with, *If it isn't here yet, then it is never coming.*

It was a natural human response to suffering and yet a grave misjudgment, which ultimately came at a high cost; many of them never made it out of that wilderness alive. They judged the future by their current season, and it cost them their destiny.

While they may have been bringing God incense offerings, their hearts were far from him, wandering into a wasteland of worry, negativity, and dark imaginings.

Their story provides a case study on the ups and downs of human struggle and the steadiness of God's faithfulness. They missed the miracle, but we don't have to.

We can decide today that we'll never bring God our slow burn of worship with our hands while abandoning it with our hearts.

We can follow a different example of traveling through dry lands—navigating it the way Jesus did.

He spent forty days and forty nights in the wilderness fasting and praying, and then the Enemy tempted him three times.

Did he react the way the Israelites did? Not even close.

Repeatedly, his responses were driven not by his feelings or desires but by the promises of God. The slow burn of his life was not deterred by a temporary dry season. The fire of his faith was not extinguished. And what should have made him weak actually made him stronger.

We can see Paul's words to Timothy in Jesus' actions here. "Fan [your faith] into flame . . . for God gave us a spirit not of fear but of power and love and self-control" (2 Timothy 1:6–7).

He can *enable us* to push back.

Let's look at how that can happen, especially considering how we can avoid the Israelites' example and be more like Jesus in the wilderness of our wait.

Weakening Words in the Wilderness

The words we choose will either weaken or strengthen the flame of our faith.

Scripture calls the human tongue "a restless evil, full of deadly poison" (James 3:8). God is very serious about our words because he knows the powerful role they play in our lives. Complaining, criticizing, and commiserating comes to us naturally, and while they may seem harmless to our faith, they are toxic to it.

Every day men and women speak an average of sixteen thousand words.[5] The book you are reading now is about sixty thousand words. So you are publishing two books a week with your words. What kind of book are you writing?

Are the words fueled by a spirit of fear and doubt, or a spirit of "power and love and self-control"?

In Miami we get mosquito bites daily, and I am the worst when it comes to scratching them whenever they itch. It feels good in the moment as my pain is relieved—but it doesn't last. Before I know it I'm furiously scratching them again and can't stop, which eventually turns the bites into scars.

I might like to think the scar came from the bite—but no, it came from the scratch. I pulled the wound open and created a larger irritation. I did not resist my impulse and redirect my focus.

Self-control is a fruit of God's Spirit and a muscle we develop more as we surrender to him. We sometimes confuse self-control with our own ability to "be good," but this is no issue of trying to conjure up goodness. It is about resolving to surrender to God and receiving what he gives—and realizing it becomes part of us only through waiting on him.

Sometimes we find ourselves "scratching an itch" in a waiting season by replaying our circumstances in one conversation after another. Is there one you're needlessly returning to that's dampening your spirit?

Maybe you are taking your worries to everyone but God, or you're belaboring or complaining about what could be a small issue if you changed your perspective. Are there times you are speaking when you should be silent?

God will give you the ability to shift gears and stop scratching so you can avoid prolonging the pain, creating scars, or even worse, causing an infection that can lead to a serious illness. Remember that it is not the bite but the scratching that can do the most harm.

Follow the wisdom of James 1:19: "Be quick to listen, slow to speak and slow to become angry." Doing this reduces the likelihood of misunderstandings and assumptions that lead to anger. If you practice patience, you will invite peace into your journey.

You might be thinking, *Sometimes I just need to vent, though—I feel a lot better after I get things off my chest!*

While this is a widely accepted mindset, researchers have found that venting actually creates a prolonged pattern of anger. In a quest to discover what really helps reduce anger, researchers at The Ohio State University evaluated more than ten thousand people in over 150 studies. The research revealed that venting was not helpful in lessening anger; instead it heightened physiological arousal.

"I think it's really important to bust the myth that if you're angry you should blow off steam—get it off your chest," one researcher concluded. "Venting anger might sound like a good idea, but there's not a shred of scientific evidence to support catharsis theory."[6]

So, are we meant to repress our anger?

No, anger is not meant to linger; it can turn into resentment and bitterness.

Should we go throw all our emotions at the person we're struggling with?

Honesty is important, but Ephesians 4:26–27 also reminds us, "Be angry and do not sin; do not let the sun go down on your anger, and give no opportunity to the devil."

Instead of aimlessly venting, bottling it up, or recklessly releasing your emotions in a way that could be hurtful, work out your disagreements or wrongs with the other person in a truthful, loving, and self-controlled way. This is the Jesus way found in Matthew 18: To work at walking in agreement, forgiving and sharing mercy just as we have received it. Whether it's anger with God, yourself, or someone else, you'll find resolution instead of further frustration.

Out of the heart the mouth speaks.[7] Our ungrateful hearts escape through our lips, just as we saw with the Israelites who had been freed from slavery in Egypt. Instead of singing the song of Moses, "God, you are my strength, my song, and my salvation," they spoke of all they missed back in Egypt (Exodus 15:2).

We might think our difficult circumstance is the quagmire we are sinking in when in fact it is our own complaining. We fan the wrong things into flame and then wonder why we feel so deflated and defeated. It is a path that leads to destroying our destiny.

The power of life and death are in the tongue.[8] When you speak to your future, you can watch it speak back.

In this current pregnancy, my fourth, I felt nauseous for the first four months. During that time we were keeping the pregnancy a secret, so I could not complain to my coworkers, family, and friends. I realized quickly how often I wanted to complain to anyone and everyone—and believe me, I would have if I had been able to speak about it! For me it was a wake-up call to the words I nearly spoke over my miracle—words that wouldn't have changed anything about my circumstance but would have colored the atmosphere and dampened my spirit.

In college I repeatedly heard a benediction that remains with me to this day. It is the words of Psalm 19:14, and it always pulls my focus back toward the light: "Let the words of my mouth and the meditation of my heart be acceptable in your sight, O Lord, my strength and my redeemer" (NKJV).

Worrying in the Wilderness

Another way we can weaken our flame of faith is by worrying. It might seem like worrying just goes with the territory of waiting—but it does not have to.[g]

A few days before Rich and I got married in 2006, when our families had gathered and the celebration had already begun, we got a devastating phone call. My nineteen-year-old brother had learned he had cancer and would need a surgery the following week.

My parents' response is something I will never forget.

---

g. See appendix for the handwritten journal entry.

After we prayed together fervently, they counseled us to continue the wedding celebration as we waited for the next week to arrive. We trusted God would heal my brother, but of course we didn't know what the future held. Because Jesus is Lord of my parents' life, we continued with hope, knowing that any other choice would weaken and worsen our wait. The wisest course was to entrust my brother to Jesus, leaving it in his hands, and be confident he would lead us day by day with the strength we needed.

We were so grateful when, months later, my brother fully recovered.

While worrying may be our default, God has a lot to say about it in Scripture.

He makes a point to dress the lilies and feed the sparrows, so how much more will he nurture us, his children?[9] There is not a single life under his care that he will neglect. Our job is to trust him with the future as we seek his kingdom first today. When we do, everything else will find its place. Today is full of enough time, relationships, and work for us to steward.

"Can any one of you by worrying add a single hour to your life? . . . Do not worry about tomorrow, for tomorrow will worry about itself. Each day has enough trouble of its own" (Matthew 6:27, 34 NIV).

Jesus spoke these words knowing he soon would be killed. His "tomorrow" held a bloody, brutal cross. He came to the earth on a mission to give his life completely—and he didn't worry along the way. Even as he was headed toward the unthinkable, he chose not to spend his life worrying.

The movie The NeverEnding Story is a favorite in our house. It tells the story of a young warrior named Atreyu, who at one point takes his horse, Artax, through the Swamp of Sadness. It is a dangerous place where depression can overtake the travelers, and some lose the will to go on. "Everyone knew that whoever let the sadness overtake him would sink into the swamp," Atreyu says. The feelings can overwhelm to the point of death.

In a famous scene Artax is pulled into the swamp until he finally meets his demise. "You have to try! . . . You've got to move or you'll die!" cries Atreyu, as he watches his best friend sink deeper and deeper into despair.[10]

Jesus knows the danger of worrying, and he tells us we have the choice not to give into it. *You've got to try. You've got to move.* The stakes are higher than we think.

It is worth noticing that we don't just worry about the bad; we also worry about the good. Many times we are headed toward the blessing and we are bound up with thoughts of *what-if.*

You can spend your entire day worried about the bad things that could happen at your job or with your family, or you can realize that God is worthy to be trusted and worry doesn't strengthen your wait. We all have to decide what voice to listen to each day. You can fear the shadow of death or celebrate the steps of life. The shadows may create an overcast moment, but they cannot overtake you unless you stop stepping forward.

There will be times an event from your past will inform a worry about your future. Perhaps today you have the shadow of a shattered marriage in your past looming over you. Or you are taking the risk of a new business with the shadow of a past failure hovering over your path. When you notice yourself drifting into those thoughts, refocus on the truth: Your past does not dictate your future, and worry only weakens your wait.

Wandering in the Wilderness

There are times throughout the wait that we lose sight of why we are on the journey to begin with. Our motivation slips away.

Our focus falters. We find ourselves roaming and getting lost, ultimately extending our journey.

Do you know how long it could have taken the children of Israel to reach the promised land? Eleven days. Instead, they wandered through the wilderness for forty years! When we wander from the ancient path, we waste time and delay our destiny.

Because a swamp of sadness enveloped the Israelites, not one from their generation got to enter the promised land except for the spies Caleb and Joshua, who trusted in God. In the same way, our own lack of faith can rob us of the very season of plenty God has prepared for us.

What does it look like for us?

Sometimes it is seeking out a new, more exciting path, not just in the overarching story of our lives but also at a micro level, such as checking our social media 450 times a day. We can get distracted, and even worse, hopelessly lost, while we wait. We ultimately will lose time instead of redeeming it and spend time instead of investing it.

Excuses are another detour that will delay our destiny, as is blaming others for our missteps.

What do we do when we sense we are drifting? We take time to reflect, be honest with God, and let him renew us.

There is a long, lonesome road that stretches across the Everglades in central Florida named Yeehaw Junction. At one point on this road, if you miss your exit, you are stuck for almost *forty-nine miles* without an exit.[11] That is sure to cause a detour, and a massive one at that. What you really need to do is make a U-turn.

When we are disappointed or discouraged, we often pull away from God and go on a path apart from him. It starts in our hearts, then escapes in our words, and before long we're going far off in the direction opposite from him. We hope for an exit sign, some kind of miraculous escape, but are unwilling to admit, "I don't want to go this way!"

Instead of looking for an exit, we need to make a U-turn. It may not be easy, convenient, or even comfortable—but there are times when you can't afford to go one more moment in the wrong direction. So what do you do? *You-turn!*

You turn and repent.

You turn and pour your heart out to God in complete surrender.

You turn and humbly make peace in that relationship.

Someone else won't make peace for us. We need to decide to turn toward God and make peace with him, right away. In one moment, we can get back on the right path with God and be headed toward his destiny for our lives.

Once we are there, how do we actively stay on that path?

Take a Long, Careful Look

The direction of our feet will follow the direction of the eyes of our heart. So we keep checking in with ourselves: *What am I fixated on?*

Psalm 119:59 in *The Message* says, "When I took a long, careful look at your ways, I got my feet back on the trail you blazed." We want to keep taking "a long, careful look" at the one we are walking with.

I grew up with 3D posters, those crazy designs where you stare and stare at the formless, chaotic art until your eyes recognize a different dimension that was there all along. Taking "a long, careful look" allows you to see something you didn't see before. Your focus will unlock a new dimension of revelation. Give yourself to the practice of soaking in his ways! He is faithful, just, and loving, and he will fill you with wonder.

The Baader-Meinhof phenomenon, also called "the frequency

illusion," is a cognitive bias that affects how we think and process information. It's a phenomenon where something you recently learned seems to appear everywhere, making it feel like it's more common than it actually is. It is biased attention.[12]

See if you can become more self-aware of your own tendencies. Are you biased toward worry and fear, and do you tend to adopt a defeated mentality? Address it before it pulls you into a quicksand of hopelessness.

There may be times when you don't know why you keep wandering on your wait. It may feel like one step forward and two steps back. Keep in mind that, when we wander, we really are searching. There is a restlessness we can bring to Christ; we can ask him to help us find satisfaction in him.

Know that your wait doesn't have to be wasted. It can be the greatest journey of your life. But it starts from a place of knowing you are already safe and secure in his hands. He is leading you on a journey all the way to the home he has prepared for you in heaven.

Isaiah prophesied of the coming goodness by relaying these words from God: "Remember not the former things, nor consider the things of old. Behold, I am doing a new thing; now it springs forth, do you not perceive it? I will make a way in the wilderness and rivers in the desert" (43:18–19).

He is faithful and will do what he has said!

Today is the perfect day to redefine your wait. You are not destined to be in a stuck place forever. You are walking to the promised land with God, and he has given you a spirit of "power and love and self-control."

Draw nearer to him, and your wait will be filled with wonder.

Rely on him as your source, and his flame will strengthen you from within.

YOU ARE NOT DESTINED TO BE IN A STUCK PLACE FOREVER.

CHAPTER 10

Make Space

R ich and I didn't talk about infertility much throughout the eight years of waiting. I don't mean we had an evasive, "silent war" approach; of course we prayed, encouraged each other, and stayed in communication about what we felt was the right approach for the season. But babies did not consume us. We had work to do, and we knew it.

We decided when we moved to Miami that we would serve a minimum of five years on staff at Rich's parents' church. Looking back, I think it was one of the best decisions we ever made—a commitment of time to sow and see to fruition. It was Rich's decision to set that time frame, and we quickly realized how much brain space it freed up for us daily (and not to mention our nightly pillow talk).

When we encountered different job opportunities—some with a better salary, larger staff, or more freedom and influence—we didn't have to waste any mental or emotional effort on it. We had already decided. So, all our effort went into doing the actual work in front of us instead of examining other opportunities.

Once when I asked my two-year-old niece Carolina Lee if she wanted ice cream, her response was, "I want options." If we're honest, our response to plenty of questions is often the same. We might be waiting because we don't want to commit. But harvest comes from sowing, from investment and responsibility.

Commitment brings clarity. As badly as we want clarity, we usually don't want that dirty word *commitment*. We see it as limiting our options. But is that true?

Sometimes less is more. Consider the practice of pruning. You trim branches selectively in order to strengthen the healthiest ones that remain. You don't allow a widespread division of energy so the life source can flow in your desired direction and, in time, cause a bigger result.

Focused energy. Bigger results. By pruning a tree, did you limit your options or increase your harvest? Both, but the focus on increasing harvest is where the power of pruning is found. You made space for the growth that would have never been possible had you not obediently cut the other branches.

Jesus said, "I am the true vine, and my Father is the gardener. He cuts off every branch in me that bears no fruit, while every branch that does bear fruit he prunes so that it will be even more fruitful" (John 15:1–2 NIV).

Pruning is not punishment. It's preparation, a clearing away of the irrelevant to produce the greatest harvest. It is a commitment to trust the gardener.

On January 17, 2012, Rich and I found ourselves at a crossroads. The weight of trying for a family had been heavy. My calendar, work, and the pressure of a race that never seemed to have a finish line was wearing me out. It was probably 2:00 a.m. as the tears fell down my face, which was significant because we didn't have many nights like this along the way. I shared with Rich that I didn't know what to

PRUNING IS NOT PUNISHMENT. IT'S PREPARATION, A CLEARING AWAY OF THE IRRELEVANT TO PRODUCE THE GREATEST HARVEST.

do. Rich calmed my fears and told me it was all going to be okay. To breathe and trust and rest.

The next morning as I got off the elevator at work, the same elevator I had ridden on my twenty-fifth birthday, my friend's mom was standing on the second floor directly in front of the elevator. She was one of the faithful Haitian grandmas at our church who I loved. Our usual exchange was a hello and a big hug, and that day was no different. The unique part this time was that she handed me a folded note, which I still have to this day. She didn't say anything about it, and she hasn't since; she just hugged me and walked away. But that note she gave me was exactly the word I needed.

Simple and practical, it read:

January 17, 2012, Prayer Time
Do not be pressured into anything you are not ready for. I have a call on your life, and you have lots of work to do. At the time appointed, not in years but like Sarah, I will visit you.[h]

God used this word to help me make space for the other things he was birthing in me at the moment. We were building our team and loving our city, and in that moment I felt the affectionate gaze of the Father on me. He was saying, *You are right on time, not behind. I've got you. Breathe and make space for what I am doing now. I have tomorrow covered.*

God knows I had been trying to cover all the bases myself. But suddenly I knew it was pruning season and that my focus needed to be refined. There was indeed lots of work to do.

---

h. See appendix for the handwritten journal entry.

You Already Have What You Need

During the first year of trying for a baby, I was shopping one weekend and saw a baby store that was closing, so I walked in to check out the stuff. I had a procedure coming up, and I was sure I would be pregnant within the next few weeks. A beautiful Swedish baby bed jumped out at me, dark wood finish and marked 80 percent off. *Woah*, I thought. *I can't pass this up.* I bought it with the mattress, sheets, and every accessory and stored it away.

Time passed and we of course had no use for that baby bed. We moved several times over the years and I had to bring the baby bed with me each time, always reminding me that we were not in a season of needing it. Eventually I gave it away because it was taking up space I needed for the season I was in at that time. I only had so much room in my home and in my heart.

I learned something big with that baby bed that set me up for the eight-year journey. *Focus on the now.* Be present and engaged, and let the *now* be your gift to your future. The purpose of waiting is not to peek over to the other side and accumulate all the gear you will need when you finally hop the fence. Waiting is about fully investing in the now, knowing that who you become today is going to transform your tomorrow.

I know that others have bought baby beds in faith; I celebrate that and think it's wonderful. But for my individual journey, it wasn't needed. If anything, that dusty baby bed reminded me that I don't want to waste any space in my heart holding bulky things I cannot use. Because by the time tomorrow comes, I may not want what I stored. I want to make space for God to make a miracle for today.[i]

---

i. See appendix for the handwritten journal entry.

Are you hoarding what you think you need for tomorrow and neglecting what you could receive or sow today?

I think about the daily manna God provided for the Israelites. He had them practice living with less, not as a pointless exercise but to lead them to the revelation of what was most important: trusting Him. We often feel anxious having to receive small amounts of bread daily—not a bulk of it well in advance—but that's what our God provides. He wants us to learn how to depend on him daily, because only he knows what is needed tomorrow. The slow burn keeps us focused on our source.

Part of the revelation you gain in the wait is that you have everything you need for this moment. You don't need more; you need to make space for what God wants to do.

The schedule gets too packed, the demands get overwhelming, and the ability to focus seems impossible. If, as we are coping, we step away from our church community, we will lose a rich source from God that sustains our slow burn in every season. But the rest of our lives is worth examining. Decluttering our mind, heart, and calendar is a constant slow burn of obedience that yields great results.

Removing the Weight That Hinders

In 1941 the American novel *Black Stallion* became an instant classic. As a kid, I loved this story about a boy named Alec and his horse, the Black. The horse and boy, each wild in their own nature, form a strong bond and begin racing as a pair. Through much adversity, the boy and his horse make it to the national championship race, and the competition with the other jockeys is fierce. In the heat of the race, Alec realizes that the only way he can win is to throw off his jockey hat and goggles and race freely.

124

Instead of trying to be like everyone else, he won the race as he fully embraced the freedom he knew was his.[1]

David was the same. When he volunteered to challenge an oversized bully, King Saul piled his armor onto David. But the shepherd boy was so weighed down by it he couldn't walk. So he removed the armor, telling the king, "I cannot go in these," and faced off with the giant carrying only his staff, five stones, and a sling. The armor was meant to protect David, but it paralyzed him instead. David had to shed the armor to fulfill the calling.[2]

This year Rich ran the Miami marathon, and the boys and I went to the race to support him. Let me tell you, not one of the twenty-five thousand runners showed up in complicated or heavy clothes. If anything, they were stripping off the extra weight so they could endure the elements unhindered.

We must purposefully remove the extra weight we carry.

As Hebrews 12:1–2 says, "Let us . . . lay aside every weight, and sin which clings so closely, and let us run with endurance the race that is set before us, looking to Jesus, the founder and perfecter of our faith."

The Greek word translated as *lay aside* here means to "lay something down and to push it far away and beyond reach."[3] The slow burn is a place to make space.

How do you make space?

Look for the empty things that are taking up your time and brain space. Decide you will stop reaching for them. Perhaps it's social media, TV shows, toxic relationships, addictions, mindless activities, or even excuses that have weighed you down. Clear those things away and focus on making a daily offering of worship and prayer so that God can make a miracle.

The Greek word translated as *weight* in Hebrews 12:1 describes a weight that inhibits a runner from running his best; it is something prominent and obvious. You probably already know the weight you need to let go of; the issue is often that it is hard to make space. But pay more attention to how much it is hindering you, and you will find a way to let it go. Eventually it will become clear that no excuse is worth forfeiting the race of a lifetime.

My son Wilde took a rough tumble when he was three and cut up his lip pretty good. It happened because he was trying to run with a heavy blanket wrapped around him and it tripped him up. There will be days when we realize that we keep tripping, and we'll need to take stock of what to do about it. Maybe we are living offended or bitter. We're living distracted or jealous. Maybe we are living for tomorrow instead of today, or we're just so exhausted we can't see straight. Release whatever it is you're holding today. Kick it to the curb. Lay it down, push it far away beyond reach, and make space for what matters.

Sometimes it's not sin that is hindering us but the pace of life that is bringing confusion. If we are too busy for God, we are too busy.

There are days that I decide my house will stay messy so I can have a moment with God. If my heart becomes clean, I have chosen the better thing. And I don't attend every function because doing so will leave me with no rest. If my calendar is full of enriching activities but my soul is left empty, I'm not enriched at all. I do not want to move fast; I want to move faithfully. My heart, soul, and mind need space for God to make a miracle.

The Miracle of Margin

Two years into infertility treatments, I decided to fly halfway around the world with friends to a women's conference. I was not speaking; I simply wanted to be in the room and take in the experience of faith. I was making margin to sit and listen for the whisper in the wait—making space for God to speak and for me to receive it.

In a session focused on prayer, the speaker invited us to turn to our neighbor and pray together. I didn't know the older woman beside me, but I learned her name was Olive and her husband was battling for his life due to cancer. I grabbed her hands to pray, and we lifted up her husband, asking God to prolong his life.

Then Olive asked me how she could pray for me, and I tried to say the very least I could, stammering that I'd like to have a family. She prayed for me and assured me that God knew the deepest desires of my heart and was right there with me. Then she whispered in my ear, "You will travel the world preaching the gospel with a baby in one hand and a Bible in the other."

It made my soul jump like a lit fire.

She didn't know that I was a speaker, and I wasn't really speaking much except for at home anyway. I carried the prophetic image home with me and pondered it in my heart. I would carry it for another five years before I saw it come to fruition.

Now, this was not the first prophetic word I had received in the wait. Countless people prayed over me during the years of waiting and declared that I would have a baby that year. I guess if I had put my faith in them and not Jesus, I could have become disillusioned or bitter. But that's not my story at all. Because every word came from people who love me, and my faith is based not on words they speak but on the steadfast words of my Creator. So often we bank our lives on the promises of others, but there's only one Promise Giver we can fully depend upon.

Turning back to that moment with Olive, I still reflect on what she prioritized that day. She had woken up with her heart heavy for her husband but also—I later learned—a sense that she had a word for two people. She was in the darkest wait with the shadow of death looming, desperately wanting her husband to be healed, yet she made space to be in God's presence. She showed up at that meeting ready to serve others.

The overflow of Olive's faith impacted my life forever. Her slow burn strengthened my slow burn, and her sacrificial offering created a fragrance that has now filled countless hearts with faith. There was peace and stability in her presence. She knew her strength came from God. This was a mark of deep spiritual maturity, a soul that has made space for the miraculous.

How can you be more intentional about creating margin in your life and leaving room for God to move?

So Vastly Wonderful

Waiting is not a curse. It's a key. It unlocks what the hustle and the hurry never could.

I find in the wait the one thing I know is mine: Jesus. And he's always proven to be enough. There is a song in my soul from my Creator. Everything else I can't control, but this melody in the night? It brings me peace and it wakes me in the morning.

There are other things—good things—that I've tried to find peace in or depend on for joy. But no one but God can be the strength of my wait.

There is a story I have carried with me since I was a little girl, and it has often recalibrated my heart in moments I've needed to turn my gaze to the Worthy One.

My parents met in their late twenties, and after dating for a year, they decided to get married. On their wedding day, my mom felt an impression from God telling her, *The moment you try to get from Denny what only I can give you, that's the moment your relationship with him will begin to deteriorate.* She deeply internalized it and let it guide her in the years that followed, making room for God to remain her soul's true source.

We all find ourselves putting the weight of our identity on friendships, jobs, spouses, children, and even ourselves to fulfill what only God can. He is the heavyweight champion of the world. Anyone other than him will be crushed under that weight. In my younger years, I tried so hard to depend on my own strength, and it only led me to living small, guarded, and paralyzed by self-doubt. That changed only when I started relying on the almighty God.

A. W. Tozer wrote, "God is so vastly wonderful, so utterly and completely delightful that He can, without anything other than Himself, meet and overflow the deepest demands of our total nature, mysterious and deep as that nature is."[4]

Let God be the champion of your life, the one who proves to be strongest over and over in your story. The one who can ground you and fulfill you. Who can speak to the deepest parts of you with love. Who has moved heaven and earth to bring you close, make you his child, and live inside you.

Redemption takes place in a moment and restoration continues for a lifetime. There is always more than we see with this faithful God who loves us. More healing, more peace, more joy, more assurance, more purpose, more revelation, more breakthrough, and more strength than I can imagine is always waiting when we wait on him.

Keep making space in the slow burn for more of him.

CHAPTER 11

Lean into the Wind

Have you ever wanted to fly? Can you remember pretending you could when you were a kid? It's absolutely wild to imagine actually soaring through the air, skyrocketing higher, feeling free and strong.

I have two little boys obsessed with flying and all things superheroes. Every night they jump off their bunk bed into a pile of mats and pillows, pretending to do daring feats in the air, each one more grandiose than the last. They know every superhero, and now so do I. Our deep conversations center around the death-defying abilities of Iron Man, Thor, Wonder Woman, Captain Marvel, and Spider-Man (I dare you to try to resist throwing a web right now with his iconic gesture). We also talk at length about Flash, Doctor Strange, Batman, Hulk, Wolverine—the list goes on!

The hero that is always at the top of our list is Superman, the OG of superheroes. He was first introduced in 1938 and has been wowing little kids and superfans ever since with his superhuman powers and iconic costume.

Interestingly, flying was not an original power of Superman; it was added in the 1940s and stuck.[1] Who would want to stop flying once they start? And are you really a superhero if you can't fly? Flying is one of the most intense superpowers a hero can have, as it symbolizes freedom, speed, and a strategic edge with a higher view.

Must be nice, right?

In a turn so incredible it could only come from God, there's a version of this we can experience in real life. Scripture promises that God will give us superhero strength as we wait on him: "Those who wait on the LORD shall renew their strength; they shall mount up with wings like eagles" (Isaiah 40:31 NKJV). It is something we are not humanly capable of or created to do—rising with wings like eagles. Yet when we wait on the Lord, we catch wind—his wind.

Something we cannot see elevates us to a great height, and up there, we can see something new. The invisible force of God's wind lifts us up to a different viewpoint, reorienting us and recasting our vision of the wait. We are reenergized when we get a glimpse of God's view and a sense of how very present, active, and powerful he is in our world.

The Power of a New Perspective

About seven hundred years before Isaiah's writing, Moses recorded God telling him: "You have seen what I did to the Egyptians, and how I bore you on eagles' wings and brought you to Myself. Now therefore, if you will indeed obey My voice and keep My covenant, then you shall be a special treasure to Me above all people; for all the earth is Mine" (Exodus 19:4–5 NKJV).

God was saying, "You've seen what happens when you soar with me; I bring freedom and miraculous breakthroughs in a moment! Remember all I have done. Keep waiting on me."

But the Hebrew people's perspective was jaded. A slow burn

was the last thing they wanted. Their ungrateful perspective clouded their view of what God had already done.

So they relied on their own strength and understanding instead of God's infinite wisdom and perfect plan—to give them their own land to cultivate, a space where they could form into a nation and their families could prosper.

At one point God told Moses, "Send some men to explore the land of Canaan, which I am giving to the Israelites. From each ancestral tribe send one of its leaders" (Numbers 13:2 NIV).

So Moses sent twelve spies to check out the promised land, and ten of them came back full of fear and dread. They created hysteria among the people, saying everyone in that land was intimidatingly powerful; the spies were like grasshoppers in comparison. Sure, sure—the land was overflowing with milk and honey. So what? There was no way they could survive there!

Their fear overtook their sight and blocked any view of the good.

But two of the spies offered a different take, looking through a different lens.

"We should go up and take possession of the land, for we can certainly do it," Caleb told the people.[2]

What did the crowd decide to do? To think like the ten spies, fixating on their own weakness instead of what they heard God say. They didn't end up taking possession of the land and went on wandering in the wilderness. An entire generation died before their descendants took the land, because they refused to trust and honor God. The people wasted forty years walking in circles when they were created to soar to new heights on God's strength.

The people didn't trust God enough to rely on him. They would not depend on his power to rise up and consider his perspective—so they wouldn't dare to imagine depending on his power to defeat giants in a foreign land. They didn't realize they never needed to possess immense strength on their own in order to soar up high or face difficult things. They only needed to trust.

Whenever you feel like those Israelites trapped in fear, know this: Waiting on God and rising up in power begins with the decision to trust.

He Has Not Put You in a Hallway

At one point in my waiting season, my fear of further pain led me to put up a guard with God. I was determined not to let myself end up disappointed. But my headstrong confidence in my own self-control was robbing me of the life and joy available to me in the wait. My self-protective efforts were keeping me from the very thing I needed to do: live freely.

This is a journal entry from 2016, when I was in that head-space.

I take deep breaths.

Kind of like trying to catch my breath on the inside because even the thought of the possibility of it happening is too glorious for words.

I pause my expectations to remind myself where my help comes from. It feels a bit like cracking the door open into a room filled with gifts, light, and wonder—then closing it shut, reminding yourself that you are so *happy* in the *hallway*.

Because of course the worst thing would be to swing the door wide open, run into the room, and allow the wonder and joy to rush over you and flood your emotions and soul, and then be asked to leave. Escorted back into the hallway. *It's not time for this yet.*

So, I protect my heart. I will experience that feeling when it is fully mine.[j]

A few days after I wrote that entry, I had an encounter with God that changed my perspective. In a worship service, the Spirit worked powerfully to shift my thoughts, and suddenly my vision was changed. I saw a bigger picture. The story I was telling myself was instantly rewritten.

I scrawled furiously in my journal as I saw my waiting season in a new light. These are the words that flowed.

The room is named the Wonder of Your Grace, and I am never locked out. I am never escorted out or ushered to another hallway. My perspective is my power.

God says, *Breathe. Deeply.* Stop holding your breath. BREATHE ME IN.
Deeply, liberally, aggressively, excessively.
Breathe now.[k]

I realized that God had not put me in a hallway, though I'd perceived it that way before. He had put me in a vast room now full of light, grace, and wonder. There I could run, dance, sing, twirl, and shout! I would no longer try to hold my breath while waiting for my outcome. I would breathe deeply and live fully.

j. See appendix for the handwritten journal entry.
k. See appendix for the handwritten journal entry.

I could let down my guard and cry, yell praises, take risks, and love deeply—all without being shaken.

Same person. Two different perspectives.

Same season. Two different perspectives.

If I'm honest, I thought my first perspective of self-protection passed as healthy. *I'm good with just the hallway. I can live small.* Yet the wonder of God is that he had an even better way for me that would bring so much peace and fulfillment.

God helps us zoom out and see far beyond our own human lens. There is so much more to the reality of our situation we can't know without him! He graciously showed me I was in a room of wonder and grace. What might he need to show you?

> GOD HELPS US ZOOM OUT AND SEE FAR BEYOND OUR OWN HUMAN LENS. THERE IS SO MUCH MORE TO THE REALITY OF OUR SITUATION WE CAN'T KNOW WITHOUT HIM!

The giants may be big, but the land is yours.

The struggle may be real, but the battle is the Lord's. He has made a promise you can count on.

Will you trust him enough to wait on him and allow him to show you what you cannot see in this moment?

It's More About the Wind Than the Wings

Let's return to the words of Isaiah: "They who wait for the LORD shall renew their strength; they shall mount up with wings like eagles" (40:31). God created thousands of bird species, yet he specifically pointed to the eagle, the regal king of the skies.

The eagle has one of the largest wingspans and can fly five to eight hours without stopping, covering hundreds of miles. They are built to navigate the skies with ease and strength.

The eagle also has phenomenal engineering in its wings, which aviation innovators have aimed to imitate. The Wright brothers, known for inventing the airplane in 1903, studied bird wings before they took the first successful flight of modern aviation. Modern air travel still takes notes from God's creation, though even the greatest engineers have not been able to fully replicate the mystery of the eagle's wings.

Small birds are forced to flap their wings quickly to stay in flight, but the eagle's wings are designed to soar on wind currents that lift it and sustain its flight. Eagles' flying technique rarely involves flapping their wings. Due to their anatomy, they can glide for hours, not because of rigorous effort but by surrendering to and relying on the power of the wind.

They utilize the wind; they don't simply work their wings.

And so it is with us. When we wait on God, he comes to us with his Spirit as a mighty rushing wind, and he lifts us to heights we could never achieve with our legs. Our might and power will not carry us, only his Spirit. "Not by might, nor by power, but by my Spirit," said the Lord (Zechariah 4:6).

Are you in a place of beating your wings, trying desperately to lift yourself above the fray? That's not the slow burn of fruition. God has a different strategy: Don't strive; soar. Patiently wait on God. When we wait, we catch wind. We can spend our whole life beating our wings to exhaustion or trust that the wind is coming, and it will start within.

We can see a real-life picture of relying on the power of the wind when God first gifted people with the Holy Spirit. There was waiting that preceded that as well.

Before he ascended into heaven, Jesus told the disciples not to leave Jerusalem but to wait for the promise of the Father. One hundred and twenty men and women decided to trust him and wait.

They didn't know they were waiting on the wind.

The Holy Spirit descended upon them, filling the entire room with the sound of mighty rushing wind. They were given boldness to testify of the risen Messiah. As tongues of fire rested over their heads, their minds were elevated beyond even their own understanding and they began speaking in other languages they did not know. People from many distant lands were stunned to hear their own languages. And as Peter spoke before thousands that day, testifying of the power of Jesus and the presence of the Holy Spirit, three thousand souls were saved.[3]

How did a moment of waiting lead to a moment that changed the world forever?

The wind.

The Holy Spirit is with you right now. He always is. Will you acknowledge his presence, even in this moment, and ask him to carry you higher?

There's a Lot That Can Happen "Up There"

Waiting on God leads us to discoveries we never could have imagined—things that God did not just dream up but already had prepared for us. And as we catch his wind and see things from his higher viewpoint, we mirror the eagle that flies not only to travel distances but also to stake out food, defend its territory, and even play games.

Like the eagle seeing its food from above, we can notice God's provision with our broader perspective. Others see walls while we see a new way. Others see *lack* in the wait, but we have a larger view that identifies what is hidden. When we are led by the Spirit, we have a new awareness.

Like the eagle soaring to protect its domain, we, too, can protect our home, church, and city through the wisdom and alertness the Spirit gives us. Maybe we have land to go occupy and overcome—some challenge to conquer—as we wait. The Spirit will help us spot potential threats and identify danger.

The eagle also flies above the storm, and waiting on God empowers us to do the same. An eagle uses the adverse wind and environment to shift higher. It doesn't retreat or run away from the adversity; it uses the elements to soar over it.

How often, when we face the storms of life, is our immediate reaction to hide, or to look to the left or right to take our cue for a response? What would happen if we waited on God instead?

He'd lead us into a way that is very different from the world's. God is always calling his children higher. To honor when dishonored. To pray for our enemies. To speak faith when the world has turned its back. To make peace when anger is the current of culture. If the current moving you is the Spirit of God and not the crowd, he will carry you higher to a place of peace, even while the storms rage.

Leave Time for Him to Work

If you're like me, you can know all of this and still come to moments when your feet are tapping, your pulse is rising, and you want to be anywhere but here. You can't help but feel ready to move *now*.

Your fingers are itching to send that text, even while you're heated—but no. *Wait.*

Time is ticking and you feel behind, so you nearly make a decision hastily—but you'll truly find acceleration when you *wait*.

You feel a pull toward an emotional response, which seems

almost inevitable—but slow down and include God. *Wait* and let him inform your decision.

Have you prayed about it? Have you asked God what he sees? He has something to say.

"Be quick to hear, slow to speak, slow to anger" (James 1:19). This is the way of Jesus and dependence on the Lord. This is how we live on earth until we see him face-to-face in heaven. And perhaps that is the assurance we need in the wait, to sense the winds that flow through earth and into eternity.

Remember, trust is the starting place. We need that to be able to wait on him with expectation. *God, I know you're going to give me a different perspective! I know there's more than meets the eye.*

We also need trust as a foundation when waiting simply means staying where God has us and standing on his Word. The disciples *stayed* in Jerusalem and waited for the Holy Spirit to come upon them. The prophets issued messages with a sense of urgency, not knowing that God intended to fulfill them hundreds of years later.

So we don't ever need to back down from a word God gives us. If he said it's ours, it's ours. The timing is up to him.

"With the Lord a day is like a thousand years, and a thousand years are like a day," Scripture tells us (2 Peter 3:8 NIV). "The Lord is not slow in keeping his promise" (v. 9 NIV).

There are some mysteries God will not surrender, and one of them is the mystery of his timing. Acts 1:7 reminds us that the times and seasons belong to the Lord. His timing is not for us to know nor is it the one thing we need most. Like Mary, who sat at Jesus' feet, we get the better portion—his presence—and it will not be taken away.

We can get so focused on the pace that we miss his presence.

He is with us, and he is active. The verse that follows 2 Peter 3:8 says, "He is patient with you, not wanting anyone to perish, but everyone to come to repentance" (NIV). Our waiting gives the Holy Spirit time to work, whether he is leading us to repentance or deeper virtue or greater boldness.

God is patiently shaping us through the slow burn, moving us to the place where we can realize the fullness of his faithfulness. Where we can receive more and more of him and be held until he fulfills every promise in heaven.

Only the Awe of the View

After God showed me I was with him in a vast room of wonder and grace, he helped me stop focusing on myself and gave me purpose in encouraging others. When I saw other people getting their miracles, he empowered me not to choose fear. I leaned into his wind and flew above the storm instead of retreating.

On Mother's Day a year after I'd written that journal entry about the room of wonder, I was, of course, unavoidably mindful that I was not a mother. I had been leading the choir at Rich's parents' church for years, and the group had become like a close-knit family, and they knew about my hope for having children. After service, I walked to the back choir room and was shocked to hear them shout, "Happy Mother's Day!" then give me cheers, balloons, a cake, and the warmest embraces. They told me that, even though I was younger than all of them, I was like a mother to them, and they wanted to honor me. Several people took the time to speak life over me, and I was deeply strengthened in a way I didn't even know I needed.

I wasn't looking for it. I was just waiting, and God met me with compassion and tenderness. You would have thought the Mother's Day cards they all signed were made of gold the way I treasured them and read them again and again.

On a day that felt empty for me, one I was just waiting to get through, thoughtful souls brought meaning and depth to my wait. It was an unexpected fulfillment, if you will, of my heart's tender longing to nurture, lead, and protect. To soar right where I was as the spirit of God lifted me above my circumstance.

Friend, do not curse the season you're in. Lean into the wind of the Spirit who will lift and lead you. Face the journey head-on. No shame, no self-consciousness, no fear. Only awe of the view God is taking you to as you glide to new heights.

Let him make you like the two spies who got a higher view. The giants didn't take up the entire lens; the giants were overshadowed by the word of the Lord. The outcome is never bound by what you see in the natural! Don't relegate God's ability to the block radius you can see.

Keep waiting in God's presence for his care, direction, and insight. He'll remind you that you are celebrated, you are seen, and your bravery to live with open hands and an open heart is worth the fight. Let love be your identity and joy be your strength.

CHAPTER 12

This Must Be the Place

Have you ever found yourself celebrating at the "wrong time"? Sort of like the real-life equivalent of shouting *Surprise!* at a party too early—or yelling it and realizing the honored guest doesn't like surprises. You feel excitement about something worth celebrating only to find out it hadn't actually happened. The awesome news was fake news. The signs pointing to dreams coming true were not what they seemed. So you shut off the party music, dial down your energy, and sigh as you brace yourself for *more waiting*.

I had a moment like this that cut deep—long before we had kids. I'd had a pregnancy procedure and patiently waited for the point when the doctors said we would see results. When the time came, I took an at-home pregnancy test and, thrillingly, the results were positive.

I ran to the closet, reached to the back of the corner shelf, and pulled out something I had saved for over a year—a tiny onesie with a Miami map on it. Rich and I celebrated with shouts of joy and a happy dance.

When I called the doctor's office with the good news, the nurse I spoke with immediately sounded annoyed. Apparently the pregnancy test should *not* have been taken yet. I'd worked painstakingly to obey every word they'd said, but, amid the onslaught of information, I somehow had missed this important memo.

"False positives are common at this point," the nurse explained. "You'll have to come in tomorrow and get an official blood test to find out for sure."

Hanging up the phone, I felt so dumb that only moments before I'd been jumping and screaming in joy. But I held on to hope that our celebration was not in vain.

The next day, of course, we learned we were not, in fact, pregnant. I tucked the onesie away and didn't reach for it again for six years. There were no more false positives throughout that time, only countless negatives.

After one particular procedure, I lay on the hospital bed as a doctor looked at me and nervously explained, "I've never had this happen before. The procedure was a failure. I can't tell you why because I don't know. I'm going to have to do some research on this. I might end up writing for a journal about this unusual case. I'm so sorry."

Months of careful preparation led to hearing, "You crashed—and you did so in grand display." I ended up with nothing to show for all that time and effort except a swollen stomach and an empty jar of Nutella as I sat on the couch, trying to figure out what went wrong.

Crashes happen in the wait—they are unavoidable. After they hit, we may feel more hesitant to respond to future news or celebrate anything that looks promising.

What we may notice is the empowering reality that we walked away from the crash—*we were not crushed* by it. So why should we fear we'll be crushed by any future disappointment or failure?

That's right: Crashes can ramp up our fearlessness.

The psalmist knew this when he wrote, "Surely the righteous will never be shaken; they will be remembered forever. They will have no fear of bad news; their hearts are steadfast, trusting in the LORD. Their hearts are secure, they will have no fear" (112:6–8 NIV).[1]

Any success is surrounded by a multitude of failures. Bad news doesn't overwhelm the overarching story of good news. Because we know no matter how bad it seems, we are truly secure in the promise of God and eternity. The fight is keeping our eyes on the reality of eternity. It's a slow burn.

A Victor, Not a Victim

I was the first of my siblings to want to have children, but I was not the first one to have them. I got stuck in the waiting lane while others passed on all sides. I remember my sister gently breaking the news to me that she was pregnant; she didn't want to crush me. It became a defining moment in my life.

Am I going to sulk and isolate and hide from the celebration of others unless I can hold my own miracle? Or can I fight through the fear? Will I let love pour out of my heart without any self-consciousness or victim mentality? I could hear my mom's words again speaking through the intimidation to the warrior inside me to "stand up and fight."

So, I decided. Just like when I decided to trust through the fear at fourteen. And when I decided to put my head down and work in Miami without entertaining other options in my twenties. This time I decided to be the best aunt and celebrator of other friends' children that I could be. I would not make it about

---

1. See appendix for the handwritten journal entry.

me; instead, I'd show up at the showers—host them even. I'd go to birthday parties and hug those babies like they were my own.

And guess what happened?

It *unlocked freedom* in me. I truly could let the love I was storing up in my heart be used for that present time—right there, right then. My love wasn't wasted or waiting.

This was not an emotional moment; it was an aggressive, confrontational moment with the Enemy. It was a time to punch the devil in the face and say, "You don't get to control the narrative of my life. I am overflowing with the blessings of God here and now." It was a time for me to learn again how to be a warrior in the wait, trusting God to bring victory, instead of acting like a victim.

This is the strength that God gives the weak when they rely fully upon him. Even if we are the weakest warrior, we'll become the strongest one when we surrender our battle to the Lord.

But if we don't completely release it to him, we will keep fighting battles that God himself has taken on and already conquered. Throughout history there have been times when wars have ended yet soldiers have continued combat needlessly because the news hadn't yet reached them. In the case of Japanese Lieutenant Hiroo Onoda, he received the reports of WWII ending but refused to believe them. He went on hiding and fighting in a Philippine jungle for nearly thirty years, resisting surrender until his former commander found him and officially relieved him of duty.[1] Can you imagine spending thirty years operating on a premise of war when it was not real? Enduring the daily pressures of war, preparing for phantom attacks, going to sleep each night feeling like a target—when no one was actually after you?

Was Onoda utterly controlled by his fear and expectation of the worst possible scenario? Perhaps. The mindset of warfare can affect us so deeply that we are unable to lay down our weapons and trust in a new season. Sometimes we don't see the small hallway the Enemy has tried to trap us in. Even in our hope we may unknowingly operate with a limit on our lives.

For me, the baby I so deeply desired was in God's plan already; he just had the due date on the calendar for eight years later than I expected. I just needed to wait. And in the wait I could celebrate.

For you, it might be the long healing that is progressing slowly but is nowhere near complete. The work you know you're called to but hasn't opened up. The sense of community that feels discouragingly slow to build. Keep waiting to see more of God's plan. And in the wait, you can celebrate.

Remember that you have a choice! Don't let the Enemy back you into a corner. Don't let him make you run to a closet and hide. Don't let him waste your strength waging a battle that God has already claimed.

The Discipline of Celebrating

In our family we have a value: *Celebrate constantly.* The definition of *celebrate* is "to acknowledge (a significant event) with a social gathering or enjoyable activity, to honor or praise publicly."[2]

Perhaps you've been waiting to celebrate; many of us do. We likely aren't noticing what is worth celebrating.

It is in times of difficulty that what we celebrate matters most—because what we celebrate, we will emulate. Think of how kids begin to value whatever we praise them for. We work the same way in our inner life. Whatever moments we choose to celebrate become the important moments of our life.

The reason the wedding is more celebrated than the ten-year anniversary is because we have decided *what* to celebrate. We all love beginnings, but that doesn't mean we should celebrate the start of something more than the continuation of it. We've simply chosen to focus on the beginning and celebrate it.

We get to choose.

Every culture that has endured for generations has celebration ingrained into its calendar and has chosen what they will celebrate. The United States lights up the sky every Fourth of July. Mexico celebrates Cinco de Mayo. Brazil holds their Carnival, drawing millions of people for parades, music, and dancing. Germany has Oktoberfest, Ireland has St. Patrick's Day, and South Africa has Freedom Day.

What do all these celebrations have in common? There is a set date and time. There was a deliberate choice to celebrate something in particular. How often are we waiting to "feel like" celebrating and missing out on it as a result?

We may have the wrong prerequisites for celebration. Paul and Silas sang praises to God, celebrating God's presence while shackled in a prison cell, beaten and bruised.[3] How do you stir up gratitude in the middle of your imprisonment? Even as they sat with intense physical pain in a dark, cold place, the eyes of their hearts found a reason to rejoice.

Pastor and theologian Dietrich Bonhoeffer celebrated two Christmases behind bars during WWII while facing his impending execution. Knowing his life would end soon at the hands of the Nazis, he still recognized the day, not just for what it held for him in the moment, but for what Christmas represented for his forever.[4]

In a letter to his parents from prison, Bonhoeffer wrote, "We can, and should also, celebrate Christmas despite the ruins around us. . . . I think of you as you now sit together with the children and with all the Advent decorations—as in earlier years you did with us. We must do all this, even more intensively because we do not know how much longer we have."[5]

Even in times of pain, celebration aligns our hearts with God's presence and brings resilience and strength.

EVEN IN TIMES OF PAIN, CELEBRATION ALIGNS OUR HEARTS WITH GOD'S PRESENCE AND BRINGS RESILIENCE AND STRENGTH.

It turns out the choice to celebrate goes deeper than feelings. It's a discipline. It's a matter of what we choose to notice and focus on.

What do Christians have to celebrate? We of course have the birth of Christ and the resurrection, but how could we spend only two days of the year celebrating when we are a people who walk with God each moment? Our roots are Judeo-Christian, and from the beginning God created celebrations throughout the year for his people. Even in the wilderness they were celebrating. I'm sure they didn't always feel like it! It was on the calendar; it wasn't wishful thinking, but the discipline changed everything.

I went to a Jewish wedding in Argentina a few years ago, and I have never seen a better celebration in my life. Grandfathers were on the dance floor with grandsons for hours. Every generation united in a complete embrace of the joy in the event. Food, dancing, music, laughter, and tradition all combined for a moment to hold forever. It came naturally to them because they had practiced it so many times. How else could it have been a tradition that lasted throughout thousands of years?

Rejoice in the Middle of the Mess

When we're intentional with celebration, we can use it as a tool to build our lives. There are certain experiences you remember and others you forget. Celebration directs your perspective. This is different from toxic positivity.

The perspective the psalmist chose was, "This is the day that the LORD has made; let us rejoice and be glad in it" (118:24).

Sounds like the psalmist was having the best day, right? Maybe you think, *I haven't had one of those in a while.* The truth is, these words of celebration were written during deep struggle. It wasn't the best day; it was a very tough time. Things were in upheaval, dreams were dead, there was a sense of losing ground, and he felt like everything was going to crumble—yet the psalmist started and ended the chapter by celebrating God. "Give thanks to the LORD, for he is good; for his steadfast love endures forever!" (v. 29). In other words, I will rejoice *anyway*!

You might want to shout that out loud so your ears can hear it. Psalm 118 continues with this, "LORD, save us! LORD, grant us success! Blessed is he who comes in the name of the LORD. From the house of the LORD we bless you. The LORD is God, and he has made his light shine on us. With boughs in hand, join in the festal procession up to the horns of the altar" (vv. 25–27 NIV). This is a prophetic declaration of Christ's triumphant entry, which we see take place in the New Testament, when people held palm branches and celebrated his presence and reign.

Even before this event happened, the psalmist was celebrating and acknowledging it. On his tough day, this was the perspective he chose. *I haven't seen it, but I can still celebrate it. I will rejoice anyway!*

You and I can do this right now. We can celebrate that heaven awaits and that, if there is air in our lungs, he isn't done with our story.

What and who are you celebrating? It reveals a lot about you. Whatever you're celebrating or focusing on is what you are building in the wait—and that also can be fear and self-pity. I speak from experience. We learn so many disciplines following Jesus, but the uniqueness of the discipline of celebration is that it is central to all of them, impacting every discipline in your life. The passage we're looking at, Psalm 118, is literally the very center of the Bible if you were to split it. The central chapter is speaking of celebration despite difficulty. In the middle. In the slow burn. God wanted us to know that the promise isn't just in the beginning or the end of his Word but right in the middle of our mess.

You need celebration in crisis, confusion, and crossroads. And you need it in the wait. But to live a life marked day by day with celebration takes discipline. It is not something that occurs naturally or is obvious. It is the result of willingly choosing your way of thinking, speaking, investing, and living. As we walk with Jesus, we learn the discipline of celebration and the life it builds day by day. We choose to say each day, "This must be the place to celebrate."

YOU NEED CELEBRATION IN CRISIS, CONFUSION, AND CROSSROADS.

Don't Miss What This Moment Can Be

Why do we always want to get through the moment to the next? We think the celebration is sweeter tomorrow, when we can really kick back and enjoy. Many of us can't wait to celebrate when we retire, instead of living here and now. And a microcosm of this mentality is the "can't wait till Friday" perspective. Just because everyone else hates Mondays and wishes the week away until they reach the weekend doesn't mean you have to accept this practice. You can't afford to miss out on the celebration here and now.

When my siblings and I were young, my mom wrote songs for us that became the soundtrack of my life, through all the highs and lows. They have reframed many seasons and moments for me. A favorite one is called "Let's Make a Memory While We

Wait." Mom wrote it after getting stuck in a traffic jam in a van full of whiny kids, and the lyrics go like this:

> *Let's make a memory while we wait.*
> *Let's not get angry for goodness' sake.*
> *Let's learn to make the most of a crummy situation.*
> *I know! It's time to play appreciation.*
> *I'll tell you what I like about you.*
> *I'll tell a funny story or two.*
> *And then you'll have your golden chance*
> *To say what's on your mind.*
> *Let's make a memory and have a great time.*[6]

Celebration is a part of building prayer, submission, fasting, and community. We would be miserable for the entire journey if we couldn't celebrate each step.

In our home, we have "Family Dinners" on Sunday nights. We eat good food, play good music, and enjoy good friends. At some point in the night we lower the music, gather 'round, and share stories of what God is doing in our community. It usually lasts ten to fifteen minutes, but it's like a B12 shot to the soul! We always say it's a party with a purpose, not just a gathering. We want our conversation and celebration to roll up in praise and glory to God.

There's a discipline to it. Plenty of times we don't feel like it; Sundays are long. But we see the value in it beyond the moment. We are building, and we're doing it through celebration. Before we go to bed after a big day of pouring out, we fill ourselves back up with fellowship and testimonies.

Something we don't want to waste time on is parties *without* purpose, where no real celebration is happening. Where there are tables full of gossip, bitterness, and frivolous, shallow conversation, and you leave feeling empty and less than, maybe even angry, hopeless, or taken advantage of.

But when Jesus has your heart and he is your message, it doesn't matter how deep a valley might be; your life has a purpose. You always can celebrate that! And as you keep focusing on his goodness, he will give you the strength you need.

The practice of celebrating small wins lifts your mood and boosts your confidence.[7] A positive focus stimulates the reward center in the brain and releases dopamine, and when it becomes a cycle, it is key to increasing motivation, confidence, and proactivity.[8]

Researchers at Harvard Business School found that those who celebrated small achievements while striving toward a goal were more likely to reach their larger milestones for success.[9] In other words, how do you eat an elephant? One bite at a time— and celebrating each bite! Celebrate each step instead of each mile, each day instead of each trip around the sun. Celebrate each time you clean the kitchen, clean out the car, or show up for that workout. It can be as simple as saying aloud "I'm grateful, God" so that your ears hear it, your mind reframes the task, and the environment is built.

Studies in positive psychology show a direct link between celebration and gratitude. Focused celebration lowers depressive symptoms and increases resilience.[10] If there's anything we need in the wait, it is resilience, and celebration is your key. Simply taking the time to write down what you are grateful for has proven to lower stress and increase optimism.

Here are words the psalmist chose to write down and allow to form his perspective of power: "I waited patiently for the LORD; he turned to me and heard my cry. . . . He put a new song in my mouth, a hymn of praise to our God" (40:1, 3 NIV).

True celebration is transformative, always resulting in some kind of exchange. Beauty for ashes. Oil of joy for mourning. Peace for your burdens. Complete forgiveness for your sin.

A new song indeed!

Redeem Your Routine

After eight years of waiting for children, I do crazy stuff. When I am changing diapers, I make the changing table an altar and I thank God that my kids' organs work properly. I may have crazy bedhead and be coffee deprived, but I'll say aloud with a smile while grabbing wipes, "Thank you, Jesus, for this baby!" I thank him for the wait and for the miracle I now hold.

Once, after I'd been doing this for a while, I set my son Wilde on the changing table, and he instinctively said, "Thank you, Jesus!" I hadn't realized that my celebration was impacting him too. You can redeem even the things that stink (and believe me, that altar is a stinky one). Right there at the changing table with a diaper in my hand I can say, "This must be the place."

Redeem your common moments by celebrating Jesus. You can practice his presence anytime, anywhere. There's always something to delight in and say thank you for. Even if you're waiting, you're not wasting time; you're investing time. You're not going through the motions; his grace is in motion. You're not waiting for the weekend; this is the day the Lord has made. Go ahead and rejoice!

"Shouts of joy and victory resound in the tents of the righteous: 'The Lord's right hand has done mighty things!' . . . I will not die but live, and will proclaim what the Lord has done" (Psalm 118:15, 17 NIV). *Resound* means to be loud enough to echo. Our declarations of joy should have ripple effects on the world around us. As we build our lives through celebration, we are influencing those around us near and far. Celebration is contagious.

One summer day when our family was leaving a restaurant, an older couple called out to Rich and me, "It doesn't get better than this! Your kids will grow up and leave home."

We laughed, and I shouted back, "You're right!"

As we parted they yelled again, "This is the best day of your life!"

Now, did I wake up that day thinking it was the best day of my life? Not at all. I was exhausted from taking care of a newborn and two toddlers. But that couple's celebration of my season made me hold my kids a little tighter. It made me whisper praises under my breath as we drove home. It made me celebrate my kids and my husband a little more that day.

You don't have to know someone to be strengthened by their joy. They made us celebrate and we made them celebrate. Joy multiplies among people!

Hidden Harvest

In a particularly trying season, Rich and I were walking our neighborhood when we noticed a neighbor picking berries off the hedges in her front yard. We started a conversation and she explained that she was gathering star cherries, which are high in antioxidants and great for health. I picked one, ate it, and thought, *How cool would it be if one day we could have a yard with fruit in it?*

The next day as I was walking with Wyatt in our backyard, I noticed a few red berries on the ground. I began to search through the bushes and, to my amazement, I discovered the exact same cherries. I had lived there for several years and never noticed them. I quickly grabbed a stepladder and a bowl and gathered our delightful produce.

Even in a season of great loss in our world, there was a hidden harvest. Pain brings new perspective, whether it is our own or we are awakening to the pain of others. That moment in the backyard forced me to examine my surroundings with fresh eyes and a new lens. To slow down to survey the soil of my life.

What had been planted? What was growing? What had I overlooked? What was still worthy of my investment?

I only can imagine how often the harvest had rotted on the ground because I simply had not taken the time to look or didn't know what to look for. The harvest is there; it was just hidden in the familiar.

I wonder what hidden harvest is right under your nose. Even while we're hoping for a particular kind of fruit, God brings other kinds our way during the wait. Maybe for you, it's building up your family members or cherishing your friends. I had a community to celebrate, a marriage to nurture, and other people's babies to hold. There are countless unexpected joys along the way.

The slow burn is the place for celebration—to notice all the good right at your fingertips and to practice recognizing that *all good things* are from him. We see God institute celebrations for his people throughout the Bible to help them keep their focus on this reality and take joy in him. This is what he wants for his people now too.

> EVEN WHILE WE'RE HOPING FOR A PARTICULAR KIND OF FRUIT, GOD BRINGS OTHER KINDS OUR WAY DURING THE WAIT.

I know you are facing hard things in your life right now. But do not forget that, even when things are bad, he is still good. And he's always available. Again and again in Psalm 118, the psalmist said, "His steadfast love endures forever."

Whatever pain you're in today, it is not going to endure forever. Whatever temptation or struggle, injustice or loss—none of them endure forever. Only one thing will endure, and it's God's love.

What might happen in your heart if you turned your focus to his love enduring instead of any pain enduring? Imagine if more often you stopped and said to yourself, *Lord, I choose to celebrate you. Your goodness is all around me! Make your joy my strength.*

Celebration brings joy into life, and joy makes us strong. It allows us to endure the journey. We may be able to start something by sheer willpower and vision, but we won't get very far without joy. We will run out of energy and break down.

So choose to celebrate not only beginnings or moments of change but also celebrate consistency, even the same old, same old. In our community, we are into "staying parties." Why should we wait until people leave to tell them how much they matter? To us, the tenth year of memories is even more valuable than the first. It is another version of choosing to celebrate the familiar.

Take stock of the blessings God has showered on you in this season. What have you gotten familiar with? Sometimes we don't appreciate something until it's gone. Ask God to help you start to see and cherish the treasure you hold here and now.

"Give thanks to the LORD, for he is good; for his steadfast love endures forever!" (Psalm 118:1).

This is the place we can see and say that. He's given us a reason to celebrate now.

CHAPTER 13

A Song for Every Season

I am someone who has become well acquainted with my lack of strength. I know how weak I am.

While Rich and I were dating, we went mountain climbing and, when I tried to impress him, I ended up needing to be rescued. Sure, I had the cute hiking shoes, but it was anything but cute when I had a meltdown on the side of the snowy mountain, refusing to budge another inch—or when fellow climbers watched as our guide had to come up and carry me down.

Another time, while riding a bike in Cambridge, I not only had multiple wrecks on my own but also hit other riders on the same day.

I once got my thumb pricked at seventeen and almost had a panic attack.

When I threw the first pitch in a softball game, I hit the batter in the back and got removed from the mound after just one ball.

Just last week I was running down the hallway and got winded. It was a short hallway.

I know what it's like to face infertility and try to solve it on my own. To be desperate to keep it private, thinking I would resolve it myself before anyone knew there was a problem.

I know what it's like to realize that the road is too long and too lonely. To feel helpless and like I'm falling apart because I'm all out of strength.

Have you been there?

God's strength becomes a reality when we realize just how weak we are.

We love to praise God for his strength once the miracle has occurred. Once we have seen the miraculous transpire—that's when we want to testify! But that's not when we see the strength of God.

We see it in the middle of our brokenness. In the middle of our helplessness. In the middle of our despair.

We see it when we don't have the answers. When there's more that we don't know than we do know. When tears stream down our faces.

When we're in an impossible situation, like having a raging army chasing us and a dangerous sea blocking our way forward.

That's what the Israelites faced after Moses led them out of slavery in Egypt. Two million people, an entire nation, stood in terror as they realized Pharaoh's army was charging after them. Inhaling the salty sea air, they saw no escape. And time was running out.

God's strength becomes a reality when you realize just how weak you are.

Right on time, God parted the sea and the Israelites passed through it safely. Then God released the sea to cover the Egyptian army, annihilating them as they crossed.

Hear this today: God is not waiting for your strength. He's waiting for you to surrender to *his* strength.

He's waiting to bring breakthrough, peace, and power to your broken heart. It's the most powerful when we acknowledge our weakness in the battle and elevate his strength.

Isn't this what Paul urged us to do? Fully depend on God because he has revealed, "My grace is sufficient for you, for my power is made perfect in weakness" (2 Corinthians 12:9).

The question is, Will you surrender?

Earlier in Moses' life, he had tried to walk in his own strength. Living in the palace of Pharaoh, Moses had tried to save one of his people in slavery and ended up murdering a man. His strength ended up leading him to the wrong place. An eruption of anger and a reckless action drove him to the desert to hide.

> GOD IS NOT WAITING FOR YOUR STRENGTH. HE'S WAITING FOR YOU TO SURRENDER TO *HIS* STRENGTH.

But years later, God showed up. He sought him and found him in his weakness and gave Moses his own strength. Moses' strength was no longer his own; it was God's strength in him. Despite Moses' stuttering problem and despite his past, God placed supernatural favor and strength on Moses' life so he could walk out his purpose.

And through him, God saved not just one Israelite but *all* of them.

Just Stand Firm

When I was a small girl, my mom would tell my siblings and me stories of men and women of faith. One of them was Corrie ten Boom; perhaps you know her story too.

In Germany during WWII, Corrie and her family were arrested and placed in the Auschwitz concentration camp for hiding Jews from the Gestapo. Only Corrie survived to tell the story. After the war ended this remarkable woman traveled around the globe well into her eighties, speaking into the lives of the oppressed and persecuted.

Corrie shared the story of a conversation that took place between her and her father when she was a little girl.

"Daddy," she had said one day, "I am afraid that I will never be strong enough to be a martyr for Jesus Christ."

"Tell me," her father wisely responded, "when you take a train trip from Haarlem to Amsterdam, when do I give you the money for the ticket? Three weeks before?"

"No, Daddy, you give me the money for the ticket just before we get on the train."

"That is right," he replied, "and so it is with God's strength. Our wise Father in heaven knows when you are going to need things too. Today you do not need the strength to be a martyr; but as soon as you are called upon for the honor of facing death for Jesus, He will supply the strength you need—just in time."

"I took great comfort in my father's advice," Corrie told her audience. "Later I had to suffer for Jesus in a [Nazi] concentration camp. He indeed gave me all the courage and power I needed."[1]

We often equate strength with advancing, having success, or breaking through, but sometimes we need his strength simply to stand firm. He empowers us not only for the push but also for peace. So many of God's supernatural breakthroughs have come after his people chose to stand firm. Moses couldn't move forward, but he didn't back down from where he stood. He spoke to the people, "Fear not, stand firm" (Exodus 14:13). Corrie could not escape the concentration camp, but her heart of faith and confidence in Jesus stayed steady.

Are you facing one of the greatest challenges of your life?

Maybe you need someone to throw you a lifeline. God will prove faithful to be your strength in the most desperate seasons of life.

- In your college season: You will stay rooted, choose to serve, and choose to seek God.
- In your job: You may be unfulfilled right now, but if God has placed it in your hands, you will value it.
- In your marriage: You don't know how to heal this, but you know you're not taking one more step backward. "In you, God, I am standing firm."
- In your parenting: You will trust the Holy Spirit and say, "God is my strength." You may not feel like you're moving forward, but you are.

GOD WILL PROVE FAITHFUL TO BE YOUR STRENGTH IN THE MOST DESPERATE SEASONS OF LIFE.

When you are overwhelmed because you can't move forward, remember there is strength for you if you just stand.

The Power of Making Him Our Song

Once we let God be our strength, we make him our song.

After God rescued the Israelites at the Red Sea, Moses thanked God by singing a song of deliverance: "I will sing to the LORD, for he has triumphed gloriously; the horse and his rider he has thrown into the sea. The LORD is my strength and my song, and he has become my salvation" (Exodus 15:1–2).

The Israelites joined in, and together they sang of their incredible firsthand experience of God. What is beautiful is that this knowledge of God passed through the generations; year after year the Jewish people continued to sing this song of deliverance.

Moses' same words appear in Psalm 118:14: "The LORD is my strength and my song; he has become my salvation." Through all their trials and discouragement, the people of God would sing this psalm, knowing who their God was!

Psalm 118 is at the end of the section of Psalms associated with the celebration of Passover (113–118) and is also read during the Feast of Tabernacles. As the last song of the group, it may have been the final psalm in the mind of Jesus as he celebrated Passover with his disciples shortly before his death.

In the slow burn, God is our song.

We offer it up to him like incense.

And if the slow burn of the incense offering brought pleasure to God's heart, how much more so the slow rise of our worship each morning and night? His children's breath in song, raising his name above every other name.

Our worship is a slow burn.

Every breath no longer simply sustains our body but joins with all of creation to fill the air with an aroma of praise. Our worship changes the atmosphere. The incense fills the air with beauty and so it is with our voices raised.

In Scripture we see "The Song of Moses," "The Song of Hannah," "The Song of Miriam," and all the psalms of David. What is your song?

Maybe there is a song that will become an anthem in your life. One of the anthems from my childhood is a Mister Rogers song; how I loved to sing, "It's a beautiful day in this neighborhood."[2] And my teenage years were dominated by every song the queen of pop Mariah Carey released. I have the mixtapes to prove it. Songs mark our lives and stick in our heads, for better or worse. ("Baby shark doo doo doo doo doo doo . . ."[3]—Now try and get that out of your head!)

Music is an innate characteristic throughout creation. From birds to whales, animals have distinct, innate, melodic songs they use to signal for gathering, distress, and other communal needs. Humans have this innate characteristic as well. The melodies that mothers often sing over their infants are called *motherese* or *infant-directed singing*. Mothers use this singsong form of musical communication to soothe infants during times of distress or to communicate emotional language like love, confidence, routine, and environmental awareness. This is a universal characteristic seen throughout all world cultures and geographical regions.

Speaking simply, all music is just vibrations of air entering our eardrums, which our brain then processes as sounds, beats, pitches, timbre, and melody. There is a correlation between "vibrations in the air" and the account of the Spirit of God "hovering," "brooding," or "trembling" over the waters in Genesis 1. Some have suggested that the Spirit's hovering or trembling over the deep could have been a pulsating or vibrating of the air, resulting in holy music.

When the brain suffers an injury such as a stroke, the patient typically retains the ability to sing. Research indicates that even when the brain area that mediates language skills is damaged, patients often are able to sing to communicate their needs, even after losing all expressive language skills. Singing can assist in the remediation of speech since the neural pathways for speech and melody run parallel in the body.[4]

God has engineered music to heal.

A father dealing with dementia and his son who is also his caretaker have connected with hearts around the world through their YouTube videos documenting the father's journey. Millions of people have watched as they sing together in perfect unison.[5] The heartwarming moments shared appeal to every age; we all need someone to sing us the song of our heart when our memory fails.

There's a strong emotional response to the songs we know.

Sometimes we forget our song in the slow burn. You didn't lose it though; it's there, deep in your soul, waiting to be sung.

Perhaps you do not consider yourself musical—but I am telling you, that is worth reconsidering. Music was once thought to only be processed in the brain's right hemisphere, but through MRI analysis, researchers are now confident that music is processed globally.[6] This means music can assist in the mediation and remediation of language, social, motor, and emotional skills.[7] Practically speaking, music is tied into our core being.

There is healing and renewal in your worship.

There is confidence and love in your song.

There is power in your daily praise.

Sing of What You Can Count On

Some of the grounding power and renewing energy that comes from singing to God is about "standing our ground" on what we know he has revealed, what we know to be true. We inhabit his truth and invite more of his Spirit, especially as we face uncertainty and fear.

Life is full of the unknown. A lot of life is spent wondering about what we don't know. *What is the truth? What is my foundation? What is the future for me?*

First Corinthians 13:9–10 says that right now, here on earth, "we know in part and we prophesy in part, but when the perfect comes, the partial will pass away." I have always looked at those verses and thought of what I don't know. What's on the other side? But I think the power and impact of the verses in the here and now is the fact that there is a part we know right now.

It's important what you know here in the slow burn.

When we make God our song, we are singing about someone we have not seen; yet we see his work all around us. We know him. And we adore him.

It is an expression of 1 Peter 1:8–9: "Though you have not seen him, you love him. Though you do not now see him, you believe in him and rejoice with joy that is inexpressible and filled with glory, obtaining the outcome of your faith, the salvation of your souls."

Our song is a slow burn. The breath of life here and now is used for his purpose. First Peter paints this slow, sacred wait with poetry and power.

I once penned these words as a reflection of this passage from 1 Peter.

The verse always romances me. I love the imagery. I love every part of it. It's the *truth*.

The last few weeks have been hard for me to decipher what is truth.

My temper swells, my mind runs, my emotions overflow. The hard thing for me right now is highs and lows I feel. But mostly lows.

I really need the peace of God. I just need to WAIT. Wait. Wait. Wait. Wait.

So, I speak to my heart. I am strong in God's strength.

I will be still and know he is in control.[m]

Speak to your weary heart today. You have a song in the slow burn. Your weakness surrendered to the Creator is more fragrant

---

m. See appendix for the handwritten journal entry.

than any perfectly penned facade of praise. As you open your mouth and sing to God, your weakness suddenly transforms to worship, and you are made into a warrior!

David—warrior, poet, and king—understood this like no other.

YOUR WEAKNESS
SURRENDERED
TO THE CREATOR
IS MORE
FRAGRANT THAN
ANY PERFECTLY
PENNED FACADE
OF PRAISE.

You know sometimes you're facing something, and you can't seem to walk it out or work it out. You can't figure it out or even pray it out. David found a way to sing it out.

If he was being betrayed, he sang it out.

If he was being tempted, he sang it out.

If he was feeling forsaken, he sang it out.

If he was desperate, he sang it out.

This is why it's important to get to church on time; the worship is not a warm-up. The newest release isn't our song. *God* is our song!

God is my rock and my redeemer.

He lifted me out of the pit.

Though I walk through the valley of the shadow of death I will fear no evil.[8]

The song of the Lord is the declaration of who he is.

God has been the song of many warriors over the years, including those in the civil rights movement in the 1960s. As the police released their dogs on little children and as they rode their horses into sanctuaries of small African American churches, God was the peoples' song. As pastors were pulled into the streets and beaten, and as several thousand brave souls marched across the Edmund Pettus Bridge in Selma and endured unspeakable brutalities—you could hear the song of the Lord. "Deep in my heart, I do believe, we shall overcome someday."[9]

We've seen how Moses and the Israelites sang the song of the

Lord after he delivered them from Egypt. *Lord, you saved us from Egypt!* And how God's people sang the same song in Psalm 118, thanking God for enabling them to rebuild and have a new start. *Lord, you saved us from destruction and wandering!*

Those words from Moses' song appear a third time in the Old Testament in Isaiah 12:2: "The LORD GOD is my strength and my song, and he has become my salvation." This time the declaration is, *You have saved us from ourselves!*

This is the same prophet who gave God's message that said, "Behold, I am doing a new thing; . . . do you not perceive it?" (43:19). God was talking about salvation even as he was referring to Egypt. *Yeah, I did all that, but behold, I'm doing something new.* Remarkably, Isaiah was holding hands with Moses and, at the same time, pulling us toward Jesus!

This portion of Scripture raises the familiar words to a higher level. "My salvation" can be translated as "my Jesus." So it can read, "The Lord is my strength and my song, and he has become *my Jesus.*"

Jesus brings salvation in every season. Salvation over our depression, over our grief, over our loss, over any situation. He's the same yesterday, today, and forever. From the beginning to the end, and every step in between.

All our stories are different, but our truth is the same.

Exodus, Psalms, Isaiah.

WWII, the civil rights movement, and every moment to come. It's the harmony of history. *I was, but I also am!* Word for word the same truth.

Sometimes we forget what we know. When that happens, we can come back to a song of trust and of truth—the same truth he's been revealing throughout the ages—and remind our hearts to hold on to him.

He Moves When You're at Your Weakest

There was a point in 2019 when Isaiah's words, "The Lord God is my strength and my song, and he has become my salvation," especially stood out to me as I was studying. I came across them in Isaiah, then traced them back to Psalms and Exodus. As I prepared a message on it, the Word became so real to me, and I sensed it was a message that was establishing my life and deepening my journey.

I had no idea how personal the passage would become to me and how it would minister to my soul when I needed it most.[n]

I was carrying Wilde at the time and had already had one serious scare earlier in the pregnancy. My hormone levels had been dangerously low, half of what was expected. The doctors were doing everything they could to help me sustain his life.

On the first night of VOUS Girl, our annual women's gathering, I was so ready to share the word on my heart from Isaiah. Thousands of women I love and admire had decided to spend their Thursday together in the presence of God. When it was almost time to head to church that evening, I started experiencing a terrible pain that lasted thirty minutes.

I called the doctor, and they said as long as I wasn't bleeding, everything was fine.

I hung up and then quickly developed symptoms that made it abundantly clear I was not fine. Terrified, I called Rich. As he rushed home, I began to weep. It was so much worse than the first scare; I couldn't believe it. When Rich arrived, he assured me over and over that it wasn't my fault.

I called my doctor again, and they explained that if we were losing Wilde, there was nothing we could do at this point and that

---

n. See appendix for the handwritten journal entry.

going to the ER would be pointless. They said that, since it was after hours, they would see me in the morning.

Our minds racing, Rich and I sat together in the bathroom trying to figure it out. By this time, we were one hour away from beginning the church service.

We began to pray. I had a hard time speaking as my tears were flowing. But then I remembered my sermon and felt like I needed to sing. I could barely get it out, but I managed to utter words from the song I'd planned to close my message with that night. "God, I look to You. . . . I will love You Lord my strength."[10] My war cry.

Rich and I decided not to go to the ER; we would wait until morning, as my doctor suggested, to know if our son was okay. And I found myself saying, "I'm not going to stay home while VOUS Girl gathers. I'm going to go preach."

I can and I will and I'm going to punch the Enemy in the face, I thought.

I got myself ready to walk out the door and headed to church.

When I arrived, I could sense the battle. My heart was focused on the night. The fire in my soul overtook every self-conscious or insecure thought. I needed God's presence more than ever. I was empowered by grace, focused on the fight. As desperate for God's presence as I have ever been.

As I walked to the side of the stage, I made a decision. *I am going to preach like there are two of us. You are right here with me, my little man.*

It was a packed house of sisters, a real community. There was an ease and a grace from the first moment.

God had it.

I preached with everything in me, and I preached to myself. *God is my strength, my song, and my salvation!* I ended the sermon quietly with reverence as I spoke on "Be still and know." I sang, "God, I look to you" as the women's heads were bowed.

Worship washed across the room. We stood, hands lifted, and declared, "Hallelujah, our God reigns."[11]

I know God had prepared that moment.

The next morning, to our relief, Rich and I heard Wilde Wesley Wilkerson's heartbeat. There were still health issues to address and pray over, of course. But God reassured us the life he'd put in me was still strong.

I often think back to that night. No one in that room had a clue what was going on inside my heart and body—because that wasn't the point. The point was that God had me in his hand just like he held every one of the women in attendance. And that's all we need. Sometimes the inner conversations, battles, and victories we have with Jesus are the greatest treasures we hold. Some are so sacred they will never be shared.

No matter what the outcome that night, I knew God was enough. No matter what the doctor said in the morning, I knew he would see me through. He had already proven that to me. Deep in my soul instead.

He is the hero. He will give just what you need, when you need it. Not a moment early and not a moment late.

God moves when you are at your weakest.

GOD MOVES WHEN YOU ARE AT YOUR WEAKEST.

He is *your* strength, he is *your* song, and he has become *your* salvation. His faithfulness in every season is a wonder that will last for eternity. May this be the story passed from your soul to future generations.

The song of the Lord holds power. Today, turn your heart toward him and see if you can say, *I can worship while I wait. The slow burn won't change my song; it will solidify it. When I don't know what to say, the song I have sung daily about my faithful God will raise a battle cry.*

CHAPTER 14

This Is a God Story

We have a papaya tree in our yard, and for months I observed the painstakingly slow process of growth. When the first papaya finally matured, I announced to the kids, "We're eating papaya today! What a treat."

My brother Dee went out with a high stool to grab the papaya, then handed it to Wyatt, who was two at the time. Wyatt brought it in, and when we sat down to enjoy it, I said, "Let's pray and thank God for giving you this papaya, Wyatt."

"God didn't give it to me. Dee did," he replied honestly. "Dee is God."

I was arrested by his words—but it *was* exactly what he had seen. I think he made it extra dramatic by saying Dee was God, but what toddler isn't going to keep you on your toes?

"Yes, Dee handed it to you, but he didn't plant the seed or water it or make it grow," I explained. "He certainly didn't imagine or create the papaya. And he didn't design the seasons to nurture it or provide the soil to sustain it."

How often we mistakenly take credit as the middlemen, thinking the story we are living is about what we have done and what we hold in our hands in the here and now. But there's a bigger and much better story that God is writing all around us and through us. We're just conduits.

Every part of our story is a God story.

We forget this, too, when we're in a terrible situation and hurting. We don't see God at work or the bigger story he has us in. We feel the effects of a broken world and how the chapter we're in has painful parts, excruciatingly difficult parts, or truly dark parts. Typically we don't know what to do with them, how to find God in them, or how to talk about them with others.

We walk around wounded and with a heaviness that can hinder us—from healing, from moving forward with our lives, from seeing how God is working actively and loving deeply.

We all have been in this place. The Enemy always will try to tell us that God has abandoned us, that there is no goodness to praise him for, and that we are caught in our pain. He'll insist our wounds define our identity and our scars darken our future.

But this is a God story we're living. It's nowhere near over.

And he is right here with us, showing us his faithfulness in the midst of pain and delighting us with his beauty. Overcoming the graves of our despair and pouring out his Spirit of power and love.

Even now, in a chapter of life that includes hurts and hard parts, why should anything keep us from all the vibrancy, joy, and healing he has for us?

Life Won't Wait on the Wounded

Throughout my childhood, my dad taught a message that still resounds in my heart today. It was called "Life Won't Wait on the Wounded."

What a thought.

To us, the wounded, that phrase feels like a blatant assault against the pain we hold so tightly. Yet it's undeniable that if you watch two people respond to their pain, they may take different paths: One may recover, and the other may never rebound. There are multiple factors at play, from the type of suffering involved, the compounded impact of previous trauma, and the resources available to them. But the role of the mindset, the story they are telling themselves, is critical.

Sometimes we make our wounds the main character in our story. Sometimes we make our pain the dwelling of our life.

We can not only walk through the valley of the shadow of death but also pitch a tent there. We can allow our heart to become bitter and calloused, convinced that our circumstance has made it impossible for any other reasonable response.

Meanwhile, there are others in our shoes who are experiencing miraculous freedom in the hands of an ever-present God.

My dad would often say, "Some folks get wounded and kind of limp through life, thanking God that he loves them.

"But the fact of life is this: Tomorrow morning somebody is going to get healed, somebody is going to get free, somebody's going to love again, somebody's going to live again, somebody's going to choose a mentor, and somebody's going to grow.

"Unless you begin to see that woundedness as the enemy of your *next*—as the enemy of your eventuality—and allow God to heal it, you're never going to be able to get into the ultimate flow God has for you."

The flow of freedom, peace, joy, and strength—which is all available in the midst of the slow burn. It can come *in the waiting*.

A victim mentality will rob your wait of its purpose. There is healing in the wait. Not just on the other side, but right here and right now. I've often seen the wait in people's lives flesh out the pain within them so they can get ready to step into their *next*.

Today may be the time to dare yourself to ask, *Is there dysfunction that must die before I step into the promise?*

As you ponder that, build up your hope about your *next* by remembering what we have known the Author of our faith to do.

Joseph once was sinking in despair in a prison cell, but after seeing more of the chapters of his story, he told his brothers, "Do not be angry with yourselves for selling me here, because it was to save lives that God sent me ahead of you" (Genesis 45:5 NIV).

God overcame their evil to build up the nation of Israel.

When Mary and Martha sent Jesus a message panicking over Lazarus's illness, his reply was "This sickness is not fatal. It will become an occasion to show God's glory by glorifying God's Son" (John 11:4 MSG).

It felt like their story had taken a bad turn.

But Jesus was saying, "Just wait. This is where God is going to shine."

The Good Story Scars Tell

A fascinating study called the Dartmouth Scar Experiment examined how people's self-perception impacted their social interactions. Researchers told the participants they were a part of a study on how the public responds to facial scars. They applied prosthetic scars to the participants' faces, and the participants saw their disfigured faces in a mirror before they interacted with others.

The catch was that the researchers secretly removed the prosthetic scars before they had any contact with others—without the participants knowing. They thought they still had a prominent facial disfigurement.

When the participants reported how others treated them with the scars, many said people avoided them or treated them rudely, which made them feel uncomfortable. Some even reported that people stared at their nonexistent scars and discriminated against them. Though participants' faces carried no scars, their belief that one was present altered their perception of people's treatment of them.[1]

A negative belief can lead to a negative interpretation of a neutral interaction. The way you see yourself will dictate how others see you. If you feel a stigma from your scars, you will carry it into every space in your life, even when it is unseen to others.

How is the way you believe others view you coming from the way you view yourself?

And what do you see in your scars? I wonder if, at some level, you might struggle with resenting them.

A scar is a natural part of the body's healing process. When injured, the body works rapidly to repair the damage. The scar emerges as the wound heals and differentiates itself from normal skin in texture, color, and smoothness. Proper care for wounds is critical to scars forming properly and without complication. In order for a wound to become a scar, protection, healing, and renewal must take place.

Do you know the very first thing Jesus did when he met with his disciples after the resurrection? He showed them the scars on his hands and side. The scars were no longer wounds but the evidence of God's healing power that overcame even the grave.

Jesus had been resurrected to *new life* and yet his scars remained. Why?

Because scars tell a story. They stay as a testimony of miraculous healing. What was once a wound becomes fully healed and serves as a reminder that the pain is gone; God proved faithful.

The scar is a visual testimony.

Evidence that the pain was real, but it didn't stay.

Proof that the battle was authentic, but what was meant for evil God used for good.

Signs That the Savior Won

There is an old Florida tale about a ferocious alligator and an even fiercer mother. It is said that one hot summer day, a young boy decided to go for a swim. He ran out the door to the water and dove in without noticing an alligator lurking in the water. Looking out the kitchen window, the boy's mother saw the alligator and her son moving toward each other without the boy seeming to have any idea.

Yelling at the top of her lungs in sheer panic, she ran to the water. The boy heard her and immediately started to swim back to her—but just as he reached out to his mother, the alligator grabbed his legs within its jaws.

The mother jumped in to protect her son; she was gravely overpowered but unwilling to let go. Hearing her screams, a farmer nearby grabbed his gun and killed the alligator.

After weeks of intensive care, the little boy made an astonishing recovery.

When a news reporter later came to visit the boy, she asked to see the scars on his legs. He lifted his pant legs proudly and then rolled up his sleeves. "Look at my arms too! I have scars on my arms because my mom wouldn't let me go."

And so it is with us. The scars of life have surely marked us, but the hands of God that held us carry the greater story. Our Savior won the battle. He is our story.

> THE SCARS OF LIFE HAVE SURELY MARKED US, BUT THE HANDS OF GOD THAT HELD US CARRY THE GREATER STORY.

Many people think that it's their achievements that will prove God's ability to the world. But often it's our brokenness and the evidence of our healing that God amplifies.

Wounds change us deeply—but so does the healing. After all, it was by Jesus' wounds that he ultimately saved us from sin. When you feel heavy about the fact that you carry deep hurts, return to the truth that God has been known to work wonders through wounds.

> He was despised and rejected by mankind,
>> a man of suffering, and familiar with pain.
> Like one from whom people hide their faces
>> he was despised, and we held him in low esteem.
> Surely, he took up our pain
>> and bore our suffering,
> yet we considered him punished by God,
>> stricken by him, and afflicted.
> But he was pierced for our transgressions,
>> he was crushed for our iniquities;
> the punishment that brought us peace was on him,
>> and by his wounds we are healed. (Isaiah 53:3–5 NIV)

Your scars point to his nail-scarred hands.

They are beautiful in God's care and a constant reminder of his faithfulness. A testimony of a healer who redeemed your life. Every scar that you carry can remind you again and again that you are so loved and there is more healing ahead.

He gets the glory for every part.

Come See His Faithfulness to Me

It may have taken me a while, but I reached a point in my infertility journey when I embraced the fact that life wouldn't wait on the wounded. It easily could have been eight years of a wasteland for me had I not come to my knees in surrender to God's plan. I could have spent that time wishing I could hide and growing dissatisfied with my marriage, friends, and season in life—all because I let the narrative of the world convince me that one thing was missing.

But instead, God faithfully counseled me and removed every bit of self-consciousness. He peeled the layers of pride and insecurity off me day by day, year by year (and still does to this day). He made me feel so safe and so protected in the middle of my wait that he then called me to share it publicly in front of tens of thousands while still not holding my miracle.

The work he did in me became the miracle.

It was in 2015, a year and a half after I received the prophetic word about carrying a baby in one hand and a Bible in the other, that I was invited to speak at Colour Conference, the very conference where I had received the word. Running for eighteen years in Sydney, Australia, Colour at its height gathered tens of thousands of women. I had attended several of the conferences over the years that marked my life.

As I was preparing my message, I felt in my heart I should share my infertility journey with the women who would be at the conference.

But that couldn't be right; no, that was the last thing I'd ever want to do. *Ever, ever, ever.* Six years of walking that path and I had never shared it publicly, even in my home church.

Why not hold off until I could testify of God's goodness in answering prayer later, once the wait was over? And with a baby in my arms too—what a moment! *That's the testimony with the right ending,* I thought as I pondered the stirring in my soul. Opening my life to people at such a seemingly meaningless crossroads seemed crazy.

I felt God tenderly remind me that I had a testimony to share even though I didn't have a baby to share.

I suddenly saw a new perspective. I had indeed experienced a miracle. A slow burn of a supernatural transformation, happening moment by moment over a span of years. God had been faithful to me in the midst of the wait. I was not anxious, fearful, or mourning. I was not living on hold.

As this dawned on me, I wanted to shout at the top of my lungs in wholehearted recognition of the sudden revelation deep in my soul. "Ah! It's always been you, Jesus! You're everything! It's always been you!"

In the slow burn of faith I found who I was in God and who he was to me. I had time to consider his ways, and he had not been found lacking. Whether Rich and I ever had a child, I had come to a real place of total trust in God and his ability to direct my life.

He was worthy of my trust. He had been faithful in every step. I was now holding his peace in the slow burn.

This was a testimony of God revealing his goodness in every season.

So, before thousands of women in Sydney, I shared our waiting journey publicly for the first time. Was it smooth sailing between the moment of revelation and the moment on the stage? No. I still had pangs of, *I don't want to be the infertility girl, God,* and, *This will not be my life's message.*

He reminded me that he had sustained my faith with his steadfast love through every step I'd taken with him in the slow burn. It was his story from seed to fruition.

One day I felt it clarified in my heart: *I can allow others to identify with my pain without allowing my pain to identify me.*

So I humbled myself and said, "God, I will be whoever you need me to be to reach the world around me," and it brought me freedom and clarity.

I'd realized that we really do overcome by the blood of the Lamb and the word of our testimony. So I chose to testify about him.

When my arms were empty, my heart still could be full. All because, in the slow burn, he is present, and his love endures.

Perhaps the greatest thing that could happen in our lives is not simply getting what we want but being transformed by encountering more of God in the wait.

Go Ahead and Praise Him Now

Life may not wait on the wounded, but God heals the wounded if you wait on him.

Are you feeling wounded today? Don't hold off addressing it as life keeps passing you by, perhaps even until your one life is over. Surrender your wounds to the Healer. He is close to the brokenhearted and will bind up your wounds. He will use the darkest seasons of your life to show you his love.

He wants to heal you today, not someday down the road when things are looking brighter.

He wants to turn the wounds of your life into scars.

He wants to create radical victories in the middle of your slow burn.

The scars you already have are not your identity nor are they your destination. They are symbols of your resilience and recovery. Proof of the journey you have traveled and the once-in-history story only you hold. Evidence of the faithful hands that have held you.

He'll use your scars to breed faith. After the resurrection, Jesus showed Thomas his scars to prove he really had endured the cross and death—he even had Thomas touch them—and Thomas went from doubting to believing.[2] We can help those who doubt be filled with belief when we, too, show our scars and testify of healing.

You always have a testimony, and when you declare the faithfulness of God during weakness, his power rests in you in a profound way. The world is not looking for Jesus in perfect lives but in broken ones he has come alive in. What can you praise God for in this season? As you focus on his character, how has he proved faithful?

It's easy to praise God on the mountaintop, but the testimony is that he's with you in the valley. He makes himself known, and he counsels, comforts, and teaches us all things. He is reaching out to you now even through creation. Psalm 89 calls the moon a "faithful witness" in the sky; it's a powerful picture you can remember every single night as you look up (v. 87). Even in the darkness God has set the moon to shine as a testimony of his faithfulness in the night.

THE WORLD IS NOT LOOKING FOR JESUS IN PERFECT LIVES BUT IN BROKEN ONES HE HAS COME ALIVE IN.

The last song I wrote before I found out our eight-year wait to have a child was over is entitled "Day and Night." The lyrics are the story of my slow burn.

You set the moon a faithful witness in the sky
Of comfort in the night
You place the sun ablaze, its glory testifies
Of the greatest light
I hear you whisper
In the midnight hour
I see your mercy
As the dawn breaks out
Day and night
You satisfy my soul
Day and night
I'll never walk alone

You set the stars in motion, all of Heaven shines
With the breath of life
You lift my head, you hold each heartbeat at a time
Your rest is mine
You are with me every moment
You have chosen to be near
You are faithful, you are able
Your love never fails.°

This is my testimony. Jesus is the miracle of my life.

Only Jesus can satisfy us. And he did it for me and he will do it for you.

Open your heart in this moment and let his love rush in. He never leaves us; he never forsakes us. He is not just able; he loves you with a love that is perfect and relentless. He will carry you through.

And when he does, don't keep it to yourself. Pass it on. Even when it means pointing to scars and sharing about wounds, because they play a role in his bigger story. You can share chapters and seasons, whether barren or fruitful. He was always working and always faithful.

Choose to say what Habakkuk did: "Though the apples are worm-eaten and the wheat fields stunted, . . . I'm singing joyful praise to GOD. I'm turning cartwheels of joy to my Savior God. Counting on GOD's Rule to prevail, I take heart and gain strength" (3:17–19 MSG).

Praise God when you plant the seed in the dark and as the roots dig deep. Praise him when a sprout grows, when the tree strengthens, and when the fruit blossoms. And even in the barren winter season, go ahead and praise him, too, for his promise of the coming spring.

---

o. See appendix for the handwritten journal entry.

CHAPTER 15

Living the Dream

O ne of my favorite things about our community in Miami is
VOUS College. Students from around the world get firsthand ministry experience while also gaining knowledge at their
university. As they dream about working in full-time ministry,
they are not always sitting at a desk; they're also immersed in
what living the dream truly is.

I meet with them weekly to teach a class called The Tension,
a name based on a quote from Rabbi Joshua Liebman: "Maturity
is achieved when one accepts life is full of tension."[1] I'm always
aiming to help them grasp that if you have an immature
understanding of seasons, you will jump ship when you feel
tensions pulling you instead of leaning in and seeing the fruit of
completion.

Throughout the slow burn, we work through that tension
and wrestle through the many moments we feel like giving up. It's
something we need to practice doing, because the hard truth is,
living the dream comes with its own set of challenges.

Living the dream is different than dreaming it.

College students across America take out huge loans, study
for four to six years, spend countless hours preparing for their
profession, their dream, only to start living it and absolutely hate

it. As psychologist Barry Schwartz once said, "We get what we say we want, only to discover that what we want doesn't satisfy us to the degree that we expect."[2]

This isn't at all what I thought it was! we think.

Of course it's not. Because living the dream is different than dreaming it.

For years I held on to the prophetic word I received during our difficult season of waiting: "You will travel the world preaching the gospel with a baby in one hand and a Bible in the other." But when I started living it, it was vastly different than a one-dimensional sentence. It wasn't a stance or victory pose to hold; it was full of motion and action!

Traveling the world with a jet-lagged one-year-old. Navigating a new season that seemed to change daily. Feeling stretched and unsure how to fill the gaps and create a new rhythm. Sensing the tension of life while celebrating my testimony. Juggling a new identity as a parent and a calling to preach the gospel. I never could have known the depth of living it simply by dreaming it.

Today I also am living the dream of marriage. Even nearly two decades in, it is peeling the selfish layers off me daily. It is stretching me and testing me constantly.

I have to remind myself, *Does your life not feel like a dream? That's because it's reality.*

Perhaps you got that new job, that new promotion, and you say, "It's stretching me. Leading people isn't easy."

Maybe you are finally free from drugs and living a life of responsibility. You are creating and respecting boundaries for your health, and every day brings a challenge.

Maybe you have a dream of restoration for your city but as you live it you are wading through the messiness of peacemaking and bureaucracy. Or perhaps your dream is establishing that incredible outreach but there is unforeseen opposition and disappointment as you seek to make it come to pass.

It looks different. It feels different, because you're living, not dreaming.

Dietrich Bonhoeffer defined the "wish-dream" in his book *Life Together*. The proclivity of our flesh is to compare our unrealistic expectations, or our wish-dream version of our lives, to the reality we live in. "He who loves his dream of a community more than the Christian community itself becomes a destroyer of the latter, even though his personal intentions may be ever so honest and earnest and sacrificial."[3]

We make our dreams an idol and it steals the very gift of living our life. We dream while life passes us by. The dream was never meant to be the idol of your life, an unattainable facade clenched by your hands while you're frustrated with what you actually see. The dream is meant to prepare you to live.

How do you avoid becoming disillusioned with the reality of what it's actually like to live the dream? You remember God is always working to transform us—which will involve tension, struggle, and finding his strength in our weakness. The tension is the wait, and the wait is life.

And you remember that he will supply all the resources and wisdom you need, however you might be feeling along the way.

When the Hurts from Yesterday Haunt You

Joseph, the son of Jacob, has been known as "the dreamer." As a teenager, he had a dream that his whole family would submit to him. Ultimate teenage power trip. His brothers did the unimaginable and sold Joseph into slavery. He eventually was imprisoned in Egypt for something he didn't do. But then he was exonerated and assigned second-in-command in Egypt for interpreting a dream!

Eventually a day came when his brothers showed up before him, begging for food for their families—and they had *noooo* idea he was their brother. Here they were submitting to him, just like the dream from decades before.

The dream became a reality, and it was not all roses.

As Joseph looked in his brothers' eyes, he felt the pain of his deep wounds, of the biting betrayal and abandonment. Instead of protecting him, his big brothers had sold him into slavery, watching him get chained and taken away to a foreign land. How could he feel anything but anger and distrust toward them?

Yes, they all were bowing before him, mirroring his dream. But that once lofty vision was now filled with deep dimensions of pain and betrayal, the raw reality of a dream lived.

Was it a dream or a nightmare?

When you realize the crossroads of forgiveness that Joseph faced to live his dream, it is truly breathtaking. Just because you are living the dream doesn't mean you won't face some moments of deep reckoning.

Joseph decided in that moment to let his faith and fortitude guide him—not his pain, not his brothers' terrible treatment of him. He declared, "What you meant for harm, God has turned for good!" (Genesis 50:20, paraphrase).

Today, perhaps the deepest desire of your heart is to live the dream, but you are stuck in the realities of yesterday.

- The spouse who left you and your children. They promised something different.
- The business partner who took advantage of you when you trusted them the most.
- The parent who you feel as if you are raising.

- The friend who ended up abandoning you when you desperately needed their support.
- The coworker who couldn't have been more insensitive to your needs.
- The boss who refuses to recognize you.

You want to live, but you are loaded down with bitterness and a jaded mentality that is changing the way you see everything.

The most important thing you could do in this moment is choose to forgive the person who hurt you. Let it go so you can dream again. A dream without God is a nightmare. Only his hands can restore you, set you free, and heal you.

Forgiveness is inescapable whenever you're walking out a God dream. No matter what your individual journey, you will be asked to choose forgiveness, and often your ability to live out your dream hinges on your ability to forgive. Because living with unforgiveness is not truly living.

When What You See Is Discouraging

What about when, one day after another, you keep having disheartening, frustrating, or daunting moments? You can't help but feel worn down as you see even more grueling obstacles ahead.

Consider this: In the natural, dreams occur at the deepest level of rest—the REM sleep cycle. In the supernatural, we find and live our dreams when we rest in God and trust him.

And it is our faith that allows us to be at rest.

We completely lean on God and let him shape our desires and direct our focus and energy. We stop striving and straining and choose to surrender and have faith.

This is not giving up. This is saying, "God, I believe you can do what I can't. I believe you are working out something good."

Your faith is not based on your perfection or ability to control a situation. It's not based on your background or status. It's based on your answers to these questions: *Do I believe that God is able? And I've seen him work wonders before; am I trusting he will do it again?*

Perhaps you are five to ten years into the plan God has for you. Friend, there's still more to come! Keep living the dream with a heart full of faith.

Relying on reason, facts, or what is seen won't work. Yes, we see signs of his hand in the world's study of science, in accounts from history, and in the order of logic. We have eyewitness accounts from those who knew Jesus here on earth, documenting his resurrection. But "we live by faith, not by sight" (2 Corinthians 5:7 NIV).

We all come to a place of deciding that we'll believe him—or we won't. When did we start thinking that we have to rationalize our belief? The dream in your heart will only come to pass when you choose to believe not in what you see but the God who sees you.

Hebrews 11:6 says, "Without faith it is impossible to please him [God]." You may have a great dream today, but God is not honored by your dream; he is honored by your faith. He is exalted when you hold on to the Word despite what you see.

American history was forever changed when Martin Luther King Jr. declared, "I have a dream!"[4] He could have muttered that quietly to himself in private and then dropped it altogether at the first sign of resistance. But what he saw in faith—and continued to hang on to with faith—*despite* the horrendous reality of racism in America, catalyzed change for generations to come. The momentum of the civil rights movement painted a vision of what could be: a United States marked by equality and justice. It all started with a man keeping his faith in his dream.

Joseph, the father of Jesus, lived a literal dream God gave him in which an angel told him he would parent the Savior who God would send. Then a series of tumultuous moments followed.

He married a pregnant woman amid the scandalized whispers of their community, having to keep God's epic plan secret. After a long journey to Bethlehem, he faced one slammed door after another, having to resort to a smelly barn for Mary to give birth in. Next, he had to flee with his family to Egypt to escape King Herod's vicious scheme to kill his newborn.

This was no easy dream.

But throughout every dangerous or difficult situation, Joseph humbled himself, trusted, and obeyed. Clearly he knew that his dream was not about him. Everything he did was for someone other than himself: Jesus. Joseph understood what it was to die to himself and live out the dream by faith. All for Jesus, quite literally. When you're living a God dream, it's about one name—the name of Jesus!

When You Feel Alone in the Struggle

To live your dream, you need faith to believe and also fortitude to fight. *Fortitude* is courage in pain and adversity, and it's something living in community helps us build.

In the 1980s my grandma had been a teacher in public schools for over a decade when she and her best friend started a Christian school. They started with twelve students, but the student count grew rapidly, and they found themselves running out of space in the little building they were meeting in.

They learned the public school system was selling some old single-classroom buildings, each strangely priced at fifty dollars. Pooling her money with my aunt, she bought seven and had them transported in a truck bed to their Christian school property. That's when the real work began.

For weeks their church family would work in the evenings and on weekends to rehab the classrooms to a state of use. They were trashed and needed new insulation, new roofing—just about new everything. One afternoon after working all day, they were so tired and about to call it quits when my mom showed up, eight months pregnant and ready to help.

She walked into one of the classrooms, her tummy about ready to pop, and put both of her hands up in the air like she was praising God.

"Hallelujah! I love a mess!" she shouted with glee.

With that one declaration, everyone's energy shifted, and they suddenly started working harder than ever before.

The fortitude to keep working as you flesh out your dream will often come from the voices around you, telling you to rejoice in the middle of the mess. You are so much more courageous when you are in the right community.

Know that, for better or worse, your community is encouraging you toward something. When I am in a pit, I need friends with radical faith! Who is surrounding you right now?

In South Florida it is a nonnegotiable for kids to learn how to swim as early as possible. So when Wyatt was one year old, we started daily swim lessons. The first day he screamed throughout the entire lesson. The next day the teacher told Rich and me, "Come outside and cheer him on."

Rich got in the pool; I stood on the edge. Each time Wyatt came out of the water, we cheered and clapped. It was remarkable how much his attitude changed! He started coming up from the water clapping, cueing us to do our job. How did he find the courage he needed to face a challenge he never had? In community. Instead of crying he started celebrating.

Beyond the faces you see around you, you have brothers and sisters of faith in heaven celebrating you too. You can be surrounded by a community of faith not only here on earth but also by a cloud of witnesses in heaven.

Perhaps you have been engulfed in tears or a giant mess. As you read this, I want you to imagine the banisters of heaven filled with men and women of faith who have gone before you. They look at you right where you are today and say, "I see you. Don't quit! Jesus is faithful! Go read the stories of our lives—his faithfulness is written all over each page."

You don't ever have to lose hope. At any moment you can choose to change the tide and celebrate in the struggle. You can be in the same deep end and in the same problem yet feel differently.

There are individuals who have tremendous courage in the face of struggles but are leaning on themselves. Their own personal giftings are their foundation, their talents are their greatest treasure, and their networks give them confidence. They may display what looks like fortitude for a while, but it can't go the distance; it's not built on the one who made the earth, who gives us all life, who is abundant in power.

If you lean on anything but God, you are trusting in something that will eventually crumble. In the end it is fruitless. But our God is never failing. Your fortitude is fail-proof when it's faith filled.

Because the story is never over with our God.

When the Timing Seems Off or You Feel Incapable

A version of this truth became clear to me more than ever when I got the shock of my life right before my fortieth birthday—when

I became pregnant with no medical help, which had never happened before.

I discovered it when I was at a hotel down the street from our home to work on this book. A few symptoms prompted me to do what I had done a million times before, to take a pregnancy test, which of course usually turned out negative.

But this one was positive.

And so was a second one.

The next day, my doctor confirmed it: I was carrying life.

I took Rich to dinner and when the tiramisu arrived, I handed him a video I'd made of the previous twenty-four hours, from hotel to the heartbeat. Tears streamed down his face as I told him, "I didn't finish the book, but we just started a new chapter."

We honestly believed we were done. *Seriously done.* God had already gifted us with more than we could imagine. Though I'd tell people, "We would love to have another," I never dreamed it would happen.

I was over-the-moon ecstatic.

And then reality started to set in. Sleepless nights. Diapers. A fourth C-section. With our youngest child now three years old, we'd finally found more equilibrium in our home. I'd finally regained autonomy in my body after going years without it. And now I'd be going back to square one.

I suddenly felt my whole world shift.

Where would this child fit in our home? How would the age gap work between the kids who are all so close? How would I fit another in my arms when I was already trying my best to nurture the three I have?

As these questions bubbled up, I wondered if I was being selfish or ungrateful. God had worked an incredible miracle in my life—and I wasn't so sure about his timing?

Have you ever been there, grappling with an unexpected plot twist while deeply wanting to please God with your response?

It hit me hard, and for several days it was a deep wrestle within my heart. But little by little, I released my expectations of what I thought the next few years held and embraced the holy genesis I sensed God creating.

He is rewriting the story. Right here, right now.

And my life is his story, not mine.

I have a decision to make, and I want to rejoice wholeheartedly with faith.

I'll choose to trust that even though I can't see this new season of my life clearly, God has prepared me more than I know and will finish what he has started.

It will be better than I could have ever planned. That's what he does.

Yes, he was putting us back in the deep end. But miracles happen in the deep. How else could you walk on water?

And the actual experience of walking on water is not a smooth, graceful thing to live out. It sounds pretty but it lives gritty. And so it is with our dreams.

As I sat in the secret place with God, processing our life change, I reflected on words from Psalm 23: "My cup overflows" (v. 5). It's typically an image that depicts the favor of God; he shows his favor like a host providing more than an honored guest's cup could hold. But when I was reading it, I began seeing that image in a different light: The provision of God was spilling over the parameters of my own capacity.

More than I could handle.

Like when someone grabs a pitcher and pours water into a glass until it overflows—and makes a mess.

But here is what God reminded me of in such a profound way: The overflow of his provision is *supposed* to go beyond what I can contain in my own strength! After all, it wouldn't be a miracle if I could contain it myself.

In this view, the water spilling over the full glass flows into a huge, spacious place, like a gigantic river, with far more capacity than that little glass.

I wouldn't be doing any of it on my own!

My trust in God allowed me to see the overflow as a miracle, not a mess. And if it does at times become a sort of mess, I know the Messiah of the mess. He always reveals his miracle-working power in the most unexpected circumstances.

And perhaps it is indeed an invitation from the Host of heaven to sit at his table and experience more of his presence and goodness. He's pouring, and I'm not going anywhere. I want his dream and I want to live in his reality throughout the slow burn.

When You're Still Asking What the Dream Is

You might be thinking, *DC, I get all this, but I'm not there yet. I feel ready to live the dream, but I don't have a dream. I'm waiting for my supernatural moment—my God word; then I will have a dream.*

If you don't have a sense of direction, you are not alone. But sometimes we feel this way when there is a "dream" right under our nose.

Consider how we see dreams function in Scripture. They were a primary way our holy God communicated with humans separated from him. He used dreams to comfort, to prepare, and to guide people; to test, to correct, and to answer questions.

But years later, when Jesus was about to ascend to heaven, he promised that he would send a Counselor who would never leave his people. And at Pentecost, God poured out his Spirit on his people, marking a new era of permanent dwelling in them.

Before the cross, dreams are mentioned in the Bible 104 times. After Pentecost, "dream" appears in only one verse, which is a quote from the book of Joel. It reads, "In the last days, God says, I will pour out my Spirit on all people. Your sons and daughters will prophesy, your young men will see visions, your old men will dream dreams" (Acts 2:17 NIV).

Before Jesus, dreams had led, comforted, corrected, and empowered. Now the Holy Spirit speaks to us in myriad ways—through dreams and through conversations, Scripture, circumstances, creation, and ordinary moments.

So as the Holy Spirit lives in you and me today, we are "living the dream" through him in every moment. We get to live in God's presence constantly, something people centuries ago experienced only from time to time when God chose to reveal himself. We're living in better days than they ever could have imagined.

Do you know what this means about the direction you're seeking? You don't have to wait on a specific God word; God has already given you a dream to live. Jesus spoke his dream for you, and it is known as the Great Commission. "Go therefore and make disciples," he said (Matthew 28:19). "You will be my witnesses" (Acts 1:8). That's God's dream. And you get to live it now and every day ahead.

Before you ever reach a goal you've set for yourself, you are living the dream.

Before you graduate or get a job you love, you are living the dream.

Before you ever become a spouse or parent—if that's your story—you are living the dream.

The Holy Spirit is living in you! You are right in the middle of the dream today. The dream isn't a destination. It's a person.

It's a dream that God himself seeks you, loves you, and forgives you, and you are living it.

Stop stalling and start walking in the Spirit. Invite him to change your life. Ask him to free you from paralyzing fear, insecurity, unforgiveness, and anger—and just watch what he will do. Ask him to counsel you, convict you, empower you, and remind you that your identity is a child of God.

How do I know he will do these things for you? Because he's done them all for me.

When the Spirit-filled disciples prayed in Acts 4:29-31, they didn't ask for a new dream or new people or a new plan. Instead, they prayed for boldness to live the dream, to speak of what God had revealed. When they prayed that way together, the place they were staying shook. And the world has never stopped shaking since.

Don't hold off any longer. Live the dream today and every single day.

An accomplished man was suddenly given a grim diagnosis and told he had three months left on this earth. He approached his time with focus and vision, investing in those he loved, saying what he needed to say. As his time drew near, he reflected on the time since his diagnosis and stated, "I was given a gift. I didn't have three months to die. I was given three months to truly live."

How could he say that?

He understood that it wasn't about the end but about every single moment along the way.

> WHATEVER YOUR CIRCUMSTANCE, YOU CAN KEEP CHOOSING TO LIVE GOD'S DREAM FOR YOU EVERY SINGLE DAY.

Whatever your circumstance, you can keep choosing to live God's dream for you every single day. Will there be moments when you feel discouraged, alone, or incapable? Of course; living the dream is different than dreaming it!

Don't let yourself become disillusioned by the way it feels as you walk. Keep on. Rely on his presence and every resource he's given you and walk in the fullness of what God has prepared.

You were born for this.

CHAPTER 16

Yes, and Amen

Do you know what the word *amen* means? We hear it and say it so much, but what is it we're saying exactly? Some folks seem to think it's the same as "hallelujah" or it's the code word for "open your eyes, prayer's over."

When I asked my six-year-old son, Wyatt, if he knew what *amen* meant, he said no.

"It means 'so be it,'" I explained.

"Well, what does *Ah-man* mean?" he asked.

"The same thing—'so be it,'" I replied, sensing the silliness brewing.

With a gleam in his eye, he pressed, "Well, what does *Ah-woman* mean?"

Chuckling, I said, "Wyatt, stop playing!"

And his giggles rang through the room.

The best definition of *amen* is in the book of Luke, when young Mary responded to the word of the Lord. The angel Gabriel told this young girl, engaged to Joseph, that she would become pregnant with God's Son. The words that came out of her mouth were, "Let everything you've said happen to me" (Luke 1:38 GW).

In other words, "Yes, and amen!"

It was, "Let *everything* you've said"—not just part of it. Not "yes, except for a few details I don't like." No, everything.

And it was, "happen *to me*." She could have said, "That's a great plan, but let someone else step up for this."

There is a version of this we sometimes do. Our hearts say, *God, let everything you have said happen to someone else who has more time or margin or ability.* We can walk into church on a Sunday and, especially if it's a large gathering, think, *Someone in here will say yes to generosity. Someone will lend resources. Someone in here will step up to serve. Someone will be committed. I'll let them say yes.*

Is that what the forerunners of our faith did? Did Noah, Abraham, David, Esther, and Mary shake their heads and say, "Nah"? No, when the word of the Lord came to them they said yes—and it was anything but convenient or comfortable.

You and I know their names today not because the word of the Lord came to them but because of the way they answered him.

Yes, and amen.

So be it.

If Mary hadn't said yes, would we be blessing a different woman who became the mother of Jesus? Did someone else say no before she said yes? Only God knows.

What about Abraham, Isaac, and Jacob—could there have been a different three-generation legacy we now call the forefathers of faith? How many were searched out and found unwilling? We don't know. We only know the ones who said "yes, and amen" to God!

Life in the slow burn is hard enough, you might think. *I'm not sure I can.*

You know what? These brothers and sisters who went before us said yes right in the middle of their slow burn.

It's possible we're not able to hear God today because the

thing we're waiting on has our full focus. But even while we're waiting, God is still speaking. It may be in unconventional ways, unexpected ways, or not at all the way we want. It could come to you in a conversation, a pastor's word, a small group discussion, or your daily personal time of meditation.

EVEN WHILE WE'RE WAITING, GOD IS STILL SPEAKING.

As I grappled with the new reality of my fourth pregnancy and the questions around it all, I suddenly remembered an unusual exchange that had happened just months before. After speaking at a pastors' conference, I came home and received an incredible text from a friend who'd been at the conference too. Her teenage daughter had heard me speak and felt God give her a word for me, but she had been afraid to share it. So when her mother found out back home, she sent a voice note of her daughter sharing the word.

"I feel like God wanted me to tell you that you are loved by God," she said. "God knows the burden you are carrying, and he understands what you are going through. And this is the last one: God is going to give you and your husband another child, and I don't know if that is going to be spiritually or if it's going to be physically, but like, yeah."

Truthfully, I've received countless prophecies over the eight years of infertility, saying, "This is the year." I've learned not to hang on to them as the only indicator of direction—but also not to discount them. I have learned to ponder them in my heart with humility and ultimately trust the faithfulness of God and the unchanging nature of the Bible.

When I heard this word, I loved it but concluded it was referring to a spiritual child. I felt deeply encouraged and carried on.

But then I got pregnant.

And the moment I remembered this earlier word I'd received,

confidence flooded my heart. I knew God had given me that word so I would know this was his divine plan. When I traced it back, I could even see that I'd received her message seven days before the conception date.

The yes of a thirteen-year-old girl to speak a word helped empower me to wholeheartedly embrace the yes of a new season at forty. For me, prophetic words are often about knowing that, before it happened, God said he would do it, and giving him all the credit, always.

Again, God is always speaking. I wonder if you would say you are listening in the wait.

What might God want to say to you today?

And what will you do when you hear from him?

His Yes and Our Yes Together

Second Chronicles 16:9 tells us the eyes of the Lord are busy right now. Do you know what they're doing? His eyes "range throughout the earth to strengthen those whose hearts are fully committed to him" (NIV). Or as Pastor Eugene Peterson put it, "GOD is always on the alert, constantly on the lookout for people who are totally committed to him" (MSG).

The men and women of faith before us were fully human yet fully committed. What does that really mean? Saying yes to the small things and the big things. Saying yes not just sometimes but all the time.[p]

When Mary responded to Gabriel, it was a big yes. But how many little yeses had Mary said before that moment?

---

p. See appendix for the handwritten journal entry.

As Jesus once said, "If you are faithful in little things, you will be faithful in large ones" (Luke 16:10 NLT).

A slow burn of obedience.

Many people are waiting around for the big yes to arrive. They want to skip all the small "insignificant" yeses and forget about the slow burn. In today's culture everything is immediate: immediate recognition, immediate provision, immediate benefits, immediate equity. But we serve a God who builds our story over time, one yes at a time.

Whatever gets your yes gets your best.

I want God to get my yes because I want him to get my best. He gave me his best. His only Son. His perfect love. His relentless mercy and grace.

He has given me *his yes*. Same as he has for you.

Just look at Jesus.

WHATEVER GETS YOUR YES GETS YOUR BEST.

Second Corinthians tells us, "Whatever God has promised gets stamped with the Yes of Jesus. In him, this is what we preach and pray, the great Amen, God's Yes and our Yes together, gloriously evident" (1:20 MSG).

Imagine *all* the promises of God waiting for thousands of years for the one who could say yes. Jesus is the yes to them all! He is the substance and fulfillment of each one.

Blessing all nations through his birth—*yes*.

Purchased our redemption by his blood—*yes*.

All who call on his name will be saved—*yes*.

Renew and restore creation at his return—*yes*.

When we say our God is faithful and true, it's because he fulfills every promise with yes! God the Father is the promise giver, and the Son is the fruition of the promises. We can say amen only through the yes of Jesus. We can say "Let everything you've said happen to me" only through the cross.

Agreeing with All That You Are

What are we doing when we say amen? We are stepping into agreement.

The Bible makes it clear that our words matter and our agreements hold power. Matthew 18:19 reads, "If two of you agree on earth about anything they ask, it will be done for them by my Father in heaven." And Amos 3:3 says, "Do two walk together, unless they have agreed to meet?"

We make agreements with ourselves. We make agreements with God. We make agreements with others. And some even make agreements with the Enemy.

Sometimes we're not even aware of what we're doing. Slow down your pace of life long enough to take stock. What agreements are you making in the slow burn?

This is no one-time decision; your amen plays out through a series of moments. When you're answering the call of God, it's for not just a season but for a lifetime. And that means your one big yes to him is a million nos—it cuts off all other possibilities. This faith is a narrow path.

When I married Rich, our vows included "forsaking all others." That meant I was not just saying yes to Rich but also saying no to every other man.

It's only you. I'm committed.
If we go through poverty, it will be with you.
If we go through loss, it will be with you.
If we go through failure, it will be with you.
I'm forsaking all others. You get my yes.

I offer this to him not just once at the beginning of the journey; I give it to him every single day. It's not that I wake up every morning having to decide whether I will be **married. It's that I** add an amen to my yes each day.

Here's the thing though: It's one thing to utter a word and another for it to come from your heart. There's momentary agreement, and then there's ongoing wholehearted alignment.

Sometimes I shop on a website that prompts me to hit a button that says "I hate savings" in order to leave a page. I will hit it—although I do not in fact hate savings. I don't mean it; I'm just clicking it to move through the site.

We can do the same thing with God. We'll say yes to him, but we won't agree in our hearts. *I'll give you an inch, but it's not going to be more than that. I'll agree with you just to get out of this situation. I'll say "I forgive" to move on.*

But when Jesus hears that, he says, "Why do you call me 'Lord, Lord,' and not do what I tell you?" (Luke 6:46).

Are you exhausted by your indecision in the slow burn?

He is waiting for your wholehearted agreement, your yes, and amen.

What is agreement? Agreement is obedience. Jesus said, "You are my friends if you do what I command you" (John 15:14). "The proof that we love God comes when we keep his commandments" (1 John 5:3 MSG).

We do it because we love and fully trust him!

It's not even something for us to question or consider. "Without any hesitation I hurry to obey your commandments," the psalmist said (119:60 GW).

My mom wrote a song that is the number-one song in our home this year, and its lyrics echo the sentiment of the psalmist.

> *Today and every day, I'm going to obey the first time,*
> *not the second or the third, but the first time,*
> *not the fourth or the fifth, the very first time,*
> *I can do it so can you!*
> *Today and every day, I'm going to obey the first time,*

> *not the sixth, seventh, or eighth, but the first time,*
> *nine and ten are just too late, the very first first time.*

It may have a childlike tone and simplicity, but this is a song for mature Christians. We say to God, *My obedience is my slow-burn offering to you, God. Day and night, when you speak, help me hear and obey. Open my eyes to what you are doing.*

All humans have the *ability* to obey. It's a matter of whether we choose to do it and how quickly we'll do it. Put another way, we're talking about our "response-ability."

Our responsibility in the kingdom depends upon the quality of our "response-ability." Pause and ask yourself, *How quick is mine?*

One of my sons often takes a tennis ball and hits it off the wall in our living room with a small racquet. Yes, I realize tennis is an outdoor sport, but I grew up with five brothers. He hasn't broken anything—*yet.* I love that he is practicing and developing his hand-eye coordination. It is the synergy of visual information integrated with the brain to create a motor plan for the body to interact with what is seen. When you see it, then you can swing at it.

But in the kingdom of God, it's not what we see that gets us moving. It's what we hear. Forget hand-eye coordination. How's our foot-ear coordination? That's the way following Jesus works. Sure, we can *see* it and *swing,* but can we *hear* it and *move*?

It may not be something we hear audibly. It may be a knowing in our heart. But either way, we are listening. And we are ready to move with him.

Trusting the Composer

Once when Jesus was teaching, there was an interruption. "A woman in the crowd called out, 'Blessed is the mother who gave you birth and nursed you.' He replied, 'Blessed rather are those who hear the word of God and obey it'" (Luke 11:27–28 NIV).

Jesus was not knocking his mother or diminishing honor. Rather he was elevating and highlighting what she did. She did not just physically carry and give birth to the Messiah and nurse him. She heard the word of God and stepped into obedience with the call. That's what set her apart, that's what made her blessed. Not that she carried the baby, but that she said yes. He was saying the only reason she was family was because of her faith.

One day I will stand before God and be held accountable not simply for what I achieved and birthed but whether I did what he told me to do. Sure, it might have been a cool plan, but was it his plan?

Obedience brings the blessing. Nothing else.

I saw a behind-the-scenes look at how the original Disney classic *The Little Mermaid* was made. The producer and composer of the song "Part of Your World" was coaching the vocalist, giving specific prompts. "Use less voice and more intensity . . . Keep it down . . . Every breath you take is enormous."[1] I thought it was masterful; he brought out the subtleties of the composition. The heart and passion change everything.

Interestingly, several online comments about the video proved that others saw it differently.

"I wouldn't have stood for that."

"She crushed it, and he still wants something else?!"

"Who does he think he is?"

I wanted to reply, "He's the creator; that's who he thinks he is. Professional singers respect the role of a composer; the song belongs to him. They're singing it, yes, but he's drawing the best for the commission. And if a singer cannot appreciate that, they won't keep the job. The role goes to the person who says yes to the creator's plan."

Obviously, Mary trusted the Composer. So much so that she followed through on her amen long after she said it. Luke's text tells us Mary responded in faith to the angel, "and the angel departed from her" (1:38).

I love that it tells us that. It is true to life now! We have encounters with God, and then it's over. We must obey *without* more manifestations or the wow factor or some kind of prodding. Conviction makes the commitment stick when the moment passes. We don't need God to check on us to make sure we're doing what he entrusted us to walk out. A mature Jesus follower says, *Less talk, more walk. I don't want a one-night bonfire. I want a slow burn that lasts.*

In our small group we host in our home, we end our discussions with prayer requests and gratitude, and one night a friend shared a prayer request that she and her husband felt God telling them to sell their home they had just purchased the year before. They wanted to pray about what to do.

Another friend in the circle lovingly and boldly said, "We don't need to pray. Obey." Then he testified of how God had moved in his own life from obedience. "Step out and do what he said," he urged her. "The blessing is waiting on the other side."

The couple put their home up for sale, then saw God move in their family in ways they never could have dreamed.

It really does make you wonder, *What might be waiting on the other side of my obedience?*

How Versus Who

There are moments we feel the prompting of the Spirit to obey and move—but in a way that leaves us asking a question that Mary asked. When the angel said she'd become pregnant, she was mystified. "How can this be? I'm a virgin" (Luke 1:34 GW).

This was not an issue of unbelief but a desire to understand. She could not see a way for the puzzle pieces to fit together.

"How can this be?" we might say to God. "I'm in no position to do _____. I don't have what it takes." You fill in the blank with your impossibility.

"How can this be? I know nothing about following Jesus. No one in my family is a Christian."

"How can this be? I'm barely getting by. I'm divorced and a single parent." Or, "I'm married and feeling the weight of life."

I'm a college student, I'm young, I'm old, I'm middle aged— we humans tend to discount where we are.

If that's where you are today, that is okay. Because if God wants to do something through you, he's going to do it—no matter how many obstacles there are.

The angel's response to Mary's question was this: "The Holy Spirit will come upon you, and the power of the Most High will overshadow you" (v. 35).

He did not speak to the *how*. He spoke to the *who*.

The Spirit of God is the one who hovered over the deep in the creation account of Genesis, overshadowing the formless void. The Spirit of God was the mighty rushing wind in the upper room, bringing tongues of fire, overshadowing the faithful with his power. The Spirit of God broke through the tomb and raised Jesus, overshadowing death.

It's always been one way from the beginning: the power of God accomplishing the will of God.

This is what you and I can count on as we step forward while saying yes, and amen.

My young kids are learning to write, so when they sit down to write a letter, I put a pencil in their hand, and I put my hand over theirs. Then I guide them in writing a letter they can't read or recognize. They are too young to understand it. My ability overshadows their insufficiencies if they submit to my guidance. They create a letter they can't even make sense of.

So it is with us and the Holy Spirit.

Scripture tells me that even my groans are interpreted by the Spirit of God as prayers to the Father.[2] He takes my wordless offerings and runs with them to the throne. How? I don't know! I only know the *who*.

The power of God overshadows us in our weakness.

When you don't know how to be a light in our nation or meet the needs of your city—the power of God will overshadow you.

When you're at a loss about how you can stay faithful and joyful or wait with a heart alive and purposed—the power of God will overshadow you.

When you're asking how you can discover the work and wonder in the slow burn—the power of God will overshadow you.

It's not the *how*. It's the *who*!

Can I Get an Amen?

We've not yet talked about my favorite part of Mary's dialogue with the angel. It's when God in his kindness built Mary's faith by telling her about the miraculous work he did.

Gabriel said, "Elizabeth, your relative, is six months pregnant with a son in her old age. People said she couldn't have a child. But nothing is impossible for God" (Luke 1:36–37 GW).

When we hear testimonies of God's faithfulness in the wait, it builds our faith and helps us say a wholehearted amen!

And when others hear reports of God's incredible works in our lives, their souls get a lift. I wonder how others might marvel about how he shines through your story—now and down the road.

Let's imagine right now that you're in Mary's position, receiving your personal invitation from heaven to embrace the slow burn. If I can "be the Elizabeth," or serve as the faith-builder to you in this moment, please let me, and listen closely.

WHEN WE HEAR TESTIMONIES OF GOD'S FAITHFULNESS IN THE WAIT, IT BUILDS OUR FAITH AND HELPS US SAY A WHOLEHEARTED AMEN!

Nothing is impossible for God. Throw your life wholeheartedly into his hands and celebrate his rescue. Tell him today, "Let everything you want to happen to me happen to me. However you will, however you lead, I am yours."

You don't have to wait for the adventure of a lifetime. It is here! The slow burn is a constant state of experiencing the overshadowing presence of a faithful God.

The world is looking for hope, and they aren't going to find it with us just shouting amen on Sunday. We need to *be it*. Remember what *amen* means? "So be it." Well, first we state our agreement, then we walk out the agreement. We follow through and inhabit and live our amen.

I'm called to generosity—so *be* it.

I'm called to serve—so *be* it.

I'm called to ministry—so *be* it.

I'm called to politics—so *be* it.

Your life is an amen in the slow burn.

Will there be moments when you feel at a loss about how to live it? Yes, but when we ask Mary's question another way—"How can I *be* it?"—we can recall that it's not the *how*, it's the *who*.

It's not our intellect, our story, or our gifting playing the key role. He is the I Am, and we are the amen!

It's our agreement that brings the anointing. It's our obedience that brings the breakthrough. All he is waiting on is our amen.

Many churches today burn incense in services, using "smells and bells" to help people remember God's grace. As the incense burns, the scent of worship saturates them. And it lingers. It is on their clothes, on their hands, on their faces as they step out of the church and into the world. The aroma of their amen has staying power. When we give that amen, it can resound again and again as we bring him our daily offering on the altar—and then transform into a fragrance the world cannot resist.

God Almighty is searching to and fro over the earth saying, "Can I get an amen?"

Maybe Wyatt was onto something when he brought up the *Ah-man* and the *Ah-woman*, because the best amen is a person—a man or a woman. Where is the woman, where is the man, who will say, "Lord, let everything you've said happen to me"?

Take a minute to be still. Remove distractions, quiet your soul, and ready your heart to listen.

Maybe you can hear him now.

I made you. I equipped you. I created your destiny.

I have orchestrated divine connections and a master plan that spans all of history.

I won't waste a moment of your journey here on earth.

I have anointed you to proclaim good news to the poor and bind up the brokenhearted.

To proclaim freedom for the captives and release them from darkness.

How will you respond to this most high God as he pursues you today? Will you give all you have back to the one who gave it all to you?

At the altar, lay down all that you can and lay it down fully. Stay in the slow burn of surrender, which says,

I'm holding nothing back.

I'm not waiting for the big yes.
I'm ready to discover the work and wonder in the wait.
  All Consuming Fire, I'm surrendered to the slow burn and I bring
the incense of my life to your fire, right here and now.

CHAPTER 17

The Wave

I grew up on a tour bus. My parents traveled all over the country during my early years doing ministry together. When they started having kids, they just brought us along. Two weeks after I was born my mom put me on the bus in a tiny bassinet, and we went on the road once again.

One time we didn't come home for over six months. There was even a day we drove through our hometown but didn't have time to stop. Can you imagine not being home for months and then heading back to it, getting close, yet not being able to walk through the door? We waved to our home from Interstate 20 as we zoomed down the road; we were just passing through.

Kinda like how we are passing through this life.

There are moments on the road of life, in the slow burn, that we get a glimpse of our real home from afar.

Hebrews 11 describes the slow-burn wave of the Hall of Faith—of people like Abraham, Sarah, Noah, Joseph, Moses, and Rahab, who followed God long before Jesus came to earth. "Each one of these people of faith died not yet having in hand what was promised, but still believing. . . . They saw it way off in the distance, *waved their greeting*, and accepted the fact that they were transients in this world" (v. 13 MSG).

The heroes of faith "waved" to their inheritance at a distance. It was a wave in the wait.

How did they do it?

"People who live this way make it plain that they are looking for their true home. If they were homesick for the old country, they could have gone back any time they wanted. But they were after a far better country than that—*heaven* country. You can see why God is so proud of them, and has a City waiting for them" (vv. 14–16 MSG).

One of the most intimate moments I have ever had in my relationship with Jesus happened while reading this passage. I had preached this text so many times, yet this time it unlocked a vision of what the scripture is communicating. It set my heart ablaze and brought me deep comfort and strength.

Those heroes of faith *waved* to their inheritance from afar. As God's Spirit spoke to me through his Word, he helped me envision myself waving to my inheritance in heaven, regardless of the outcome of my journey here.

I waved to it and wept.

Suddenly I could see that my journey was not just my present season and not just this life. I had so much to look forward to, and the eyes of my heart could see it.

Could it be that a revelation of eternity is what we need to walk out our daily faith in a broken world? That this wave from a distance is not just a promise for tomorrow but faith for today?

A Life Shaped by His Faithfulness

The holiday season in Miami is beautiful. Each year as I step into stores to find gifts for loved ones, I always am amazed at the brilliant sales techniques on display. Each sign promises an item will delight and satisfy, conveying one way or the other, *This is what everyone wants. This is the ultimate thing.*

But what if someone told you the gift they offered was never having another problem? No more tears, never longing for anything, never being sick again, no more brokenness or pain. Only fulfillment and the most euphoric joy and purpose. It's the gift of no more waiting in the slow burn. Seeing Jesus face-to-face and dwelling in his presence. Forever.

It sounds too good to be true, but it is the promise we hold and greet from afar.

Eric Clapton wrote the song "Tears in Heaven" after tragically losing his young son. His grief, vulnerability, and honest questions reverberated around the world. Clapton questioned if he had a place in eternity, saying, "I don't belong," only to conclude, "Beyond the door, there's peace, I'm sure. 'Cause I know there'll be no more tears in heaven."[1]

Our humanity struggles to understand a perfection we have never known. Yet through Jesus we all can belong and know the reality of a very real heaven.

This is the gift of eternal life from the giver of all, God the Father.

Can we, like our matriarchs and patriarchs of faith, accept the fact that our momentary troubles will not endure, but his love endures forever? They didn't receive their inheritance on this side of eternity. They died when they were still in the slow burn—but as they waited, they waved to all that beauty ahead.

The hard question is this: What if the thing you want so desperately never comes true?

What if you never get the dream job, never find a partner, never get full healing, never have a child?

I want to speak strength to your soul. *Your life will not be wasted in the wait.* If Jesus is Lord, your life *will* be shaped by his faithfulness.

God always answers prayer. He says yes, no, and wait. That is what lordship is about.

Do you want to know what the testimony of your life will be if you stay steady in the slow burn? I can tell you.

> *I waited on God, and I saw his faithfulness.*
>
> *I waited on God, and I saw his providence.*
>
> *I waited on God, and I saw his protection.*
>
> *Perhaps it was a no this side of heaven, but I know that he is near.*
>
> *A no in the now is not a rejection or a final word.*

GOD ALWAYS ANSWERS PRAYER. HE SAYS YES, NO, AND WAIT.

Understand this: From the moment you surrender your life to Jesus you are a citizen of the kingdom of God. It is not *if* the slow burn will end; it is *when*. And when it does, you'll be stepping into a beautiful future.

One of thirteen children, my grandfather was born into dire poverty in 1912. Crisis hit his family when his mother was diagnosed with terminal brain tumors and was told she had only months to live. Amid her devastation and worries about her children's future without her, she was invited to a tent revival and, having no other hope, she decided to attend.

As the pastor prayed that night, God radically healed her.

She went on to live for decades, and all of her children followed Jesus because of her beautiful faith.

My grandfather, who I called Papa, went into ministry at a young age—and at a high cost. He and my grandma went from city to city preaching the gospel, owning only what could fit in the trunk of their car and raising their young son—my father—on the road.

They eventually put down roots in Shreveport, Louisiana, and pastored there for over forty years. My father followed in Papa's footsteps, and now my brother is doing the same. It's the community that raised me.

Papa was bilingual, and he'd often slip into his native Cajun French when speaking in American English, his second language. Though his sermons were not eloquent, people would fill the altars every week as he shared the love of Jesus with passion and conviction. He also went to hospitals daily to pray for people; it became the place he was most comfortable praying for folks. He was a pastor not only to a congregation but to a city.

Over his eighty-eight years of life, Papa walked through grief, deep pain, and failure. Yet whenever he came home in the evening, heavy with a bad report and a feeling of futility, he would hit a point when he'd say, "Oh shoot! I'm not gonna worry about that!" Then he'd run to the piano and sing his favorite hymn at the top of his lungs. "For many a year I traveled life's pathways, sharing its joy, its sorrow and pain . . . and it's just about time for me to lay down my cross and go home."[2]

What a way to wave!

As Papa worshiped in faith, looking toward the future only the eyes of his soul could see, he was filled with more faith for today. God was his strength, song, and salvation. The wave shifted him out of momentary despair and gave him strength for the slow burn. He went from feeling stuck within the confines of the current moment to feeling empowered to move forward.

He waved again and again through every season of his life, and now he is face-to-face with Jesus.

And as eternity held his heart, his life message was, *The best is yet to come.*

How often do you think about heaven—really think about it? And have you ever waved?

The Glory He'll Have for Us

Let's back up. What is heaven? What does eternity hold?

Our pictures of heaven come from fairy tales, little angels in diapers flying around the clouds. But God's Word is real and so much more robust.

Heaven is where God most fully makes his presence known to bless. Eternity is a place, not just a state of mind. Jesus, as he ascended, told us, "I go to prepare a place for you" (John 14:2). The entire point of this dialogue is the place.

Our bodies in heaven will be our resurrected bodies. They will never grow old, weak, or ill. Brought back to the perfect creation he first established when he said, "It is good." We will eat and drink at the marriage supper of the Lamb. (My mom always says the Italians will oversee this meal—and I'd be good with that!)

There will be a new heaven and a new earth. Yes, a new earth. As N. T. Wright said, "Heaven is important but it's not the end of the world."[3] Heaven and earth will be renewed, made whole, complete and perfect. It is the enduring love of the Father that will make all things new.

I love Pastor Eugene Peterson's take on John's vision of heaven in Revelation:

I saw Heaven and earth new-created. Gone the first Heaven, gone the first earth, gone the sea. I saw Holy Jerusalem, new-created, descending resplendent out of Heaven, as ready for God as a bride for her husband. I heard a voice thunder from the Throne: "Look! Look! God has moved into the neighborhood, making his home with men and women! They're his people, he's their God. He'll wipe every tear from their eyes. Death is gone for good—tears gone, crying gone, pain gone—all the first order of things gone." The Enthroned continued, "Look! I'm making everything new. Write it all down—each word dependable and accurate." (21:1–5 MSG)

This vision is only a small glimpse of the glory awaiting us. It is pure. Pure love that the world has never seen. Nothing missing and nothing broken. The shalom peace of God reigning forever. All because of Jesus.

The best part? We will have unhindered fellowship with God. Everything we search for in the slow burn is found in his presence.

Neuroscientist Caroline Leaf said, "We are designed to be addicted to God."[4] By design, we all have a longing that can't be fulfilled here on earth. That is the power of "the wave." We are looking over with love, connecting however we can from here to where we truly belong. And as we do, we get to see some of its glory shining through and experience bits of its deep goodness in our souls.

As believers heaven should hold our hearts—not just because it is bursting with beauty, but because we are united with Jesus now. It is the expansion of the communion we have with him and the ultimate expression of the new creation he's made us to be. Everything about our identity is not of this life or world but of the next.

Our *Father* is in heaven. Jesus prayed with the disciples, "Our Father in heaven" (Matthew 6:9).

Our *Savior* is in heaven making intercession for us.

Our *name* is in heaven, written in the Lamb's Book of Life.

Paul testified, "Our *citizenship* is in heaven" (Philippians 3:20).

Our *home* is in heaven. Jesus said, "In my Father's house are many rooms. If it were not so, would I have told you that I go to prepare a place for you? And if I go and prepare a place for you,

I will come again and will take you to myself, that where I am you may be also" (John 14:2–3).

Our *inheritance* is in heaven. It is "an inheritance that is imperishable, undefiled, and unfading, kept in heaven for you" (1 Peter 1:4).

Our *heart* is meant to be in eternity with Jesus. "Where your treasure is, there your heart will be also," he said (Matthew 6:21).

Take a minute to gather all of this in your mind and in your soul, and let it sink in. Sit with the wonder of what he's done. The reality he has created for you, both today and tomorrow. The true life and wholeness he invites you into. Maybe as you do, you'll want to grab a journal and write something like I did years ago.

> As surely as I sit today with pen and paper within my temporary home, one day I will stand before my Father and my Savior in Heaven. It will be my reality. Lord, let me focus on the unseen, that which is the supply of heaven.
>
> *Pause.*
>
> The day will come.[q]

Eternal Storehouse and Living on Mission

When our Creator gives us a preview of heaven, he's not only encouraging our hearts to keep moving toward our perfect home with him. He's also calling us to impact eternity with our lives in the present. God plants a seed of eternity in our hearts that is full of potential and establishes our true identity, so we know our true purpose.

---

q. See appendix for the handwritten journal entry.

Jesus once said, "Do not lay up for yourselves treasures on earth, where moth and rust destroy and where thieves break in and steal, but lay up for yourselves treasures in heaven, where neither moth nor rust destroys and where thieves do not break in and steal" (Matthew 6:19–20).

Today Jesus asks you, "Where is your storehouse?"

You probably have heard the phrase, "You'll never see a U-Haul behind a hearse." None of our possessions are going with us! We're meant to use possessions and love people, not love possessions and use people. When we do, it sends a powerful message to those around us. It's a fragrant aroma that our culture can't comprehend and the world can't supply.

It is so easy to forget that your slow burn has an expiration date, but it's true. One day your home will crumble, and your cars will rust. Your clothes and shoes will be gone, and your wealth and status will fade from memory. But your investment into the kingdom of God will not return void.

Your eternal perspective will impact your earthly priorities. Steward, plan, save—yes. But know that God is the only sure foundation to place your life upon. All the rest can be gone in a moment.

Notice that Jesus did not stop at saying we shouldn't store treasures on earth. He also said, "Lay up for yourselves treasures in heaven, where neither moth nor rust destroys and where thieves do not break in and steal" (v. 20).

Jesus is the best investment adviser you could ever have and he's telling you where your portfolio belongs. Where is your treasure? How is that seen in how you live, and how does it impact those around you?

C. S. Lewis wrote in *Mere Christianity*: "If you read history, you will find that the Christians who did the most for the present world were just those who thought most of the next. . . . It is since

Christians have largely ceased to think of the other world that they have become so ineffective in this."[5]

Around the world a revival is taking place. CEOs are offering their gifts to build God's kingdom. Artists are collaborating for the glory of God. Single parents, entrepreneurs, college students, grandparents, trendsetters, and everyone in between are awakening to their purpose!

With every wave we recognize the reality of heaven, and it compels radical obedience today.

It also fills us with joy, giving us a glimmer of the fullness of joy ahead.

There is a beautiful picture of this in the life of Ludwig van Beethoven, whom many consider the greatest composer of all time. He began losing his hearing in his twenties and was completely deaf by age forty-five. Several years later he began working on one of his greatest works, the Ninth Symphony, despite being unable to hear the notations he was creating.

Beethoven utilized Friedrich Schiller's poem "Ode to Joy" for the work. It was a piece Schiller had revised repeatedly throughout his life; he'd never been truly satisfied with it and died thinking it was a failure. But the message of brotherhood and unity in the poem spoke to Beethoven's core.

As the great composer wrestled with his own tragic battle, wars raged around the world; he could not escape the conflict within him or around him. Yet he persevered against impossible odds, composing a masterpiece without the ability to ever hear it himself—a masterpiece that has stood the test of time for two hundred years.

"Day by day I am approaching the goal which I apprehend but cannot describe," he wrote as he worked on it.[6]

When his "Symphony No. 9 in D Minor, Op. 125" was performed for the first time in 1824, Beethoven broke new ground by featuring voices in the final movement, singing the refrain of

Schiller's poem "Ode to Joy." Beethoven insisted on conducting the performance himself, though he could not hear a thing.

Pause for a moment and take that in.

He stood waving his baton to a symphony he could only imagine and truly hear with his heart. His current reality was a slow burn of suffering, yet with every wave of his baton, his fierce focus and declaration in the wait was an "Ode to Joy."

As it ended, the audience erupted in immediate praise, recognizing Beethoven's brilliance and persistence to overcome the obstacles he'd faced. "Encore, encore!" every voice called out, adamantly requesting to hear it "again, again!"

Could Beethoven have ever dreamed that, to this day, the beauty he brought in his wait would be played again and again?

After Beethoven's death, Henry van Dyke put his poetry to Beethoven's melody, creating a new iteration known as "The Hymn of Joy" or "Joyful, Joyful We Adore Thee." It became an anthem for the ages. Schiller, Beethoven, and van Dyke died not knowing the next generation would build off their contribution.

In Romans 15, Paul described believers living unified in Jesus, and here's how *The Message* interprets it: "We'll be a choir—not our voices only, but our very lives singing in harmony in a stunning anthem to the God and Father of our Master Jesus!" (v. 6). While Beethoven shattered the definition of a symphony by adding human voices, God has allowed us, through his Son shattering the curse of sin, to add our voices to his symphony of salvation. With his Spirit in us, we lift holy hands and acknowledge the coming fullness of joy.

And as we wave to our inheritance from afar and even die while still believing in faith, we can sing:

Melt the clouds of sin and sadness,
Drive the dark of doubt away.

Giver of immortal gladness,
Fill us with the light of day.

We know that ahead of us is an eternal encore of joy, one that will outlast all the waiting of this world. Again and again and for all eternity, we will bask in his endless love.

Your slow burn will not end as a song of suffering; it will be a hymn of joy.

Waving Together

Rich and I once hosted a conference with thousands of people, and five minutes before it was supposed to begin, the power went out. It felt like a moment that could set the tone of the entire event, and I braced myself for some kind of mass awkwardness as everyone waited in silence.

But something entirely different happened instead.

One brave soul jumped to their feet, threw their arms up in the air, and enthusiastically moved their hands from side to side. This spurred people around them to do the same. Before we knew it, every person in the arena wasn't simply waiting; they were participating.

It was *the wave.*

This wasn't just bodies moving; it was joy and energy rolling like waves through the entire place. Every age, background, and story united in a synchronized acknowledgment of one another. A heartfelt collective celebration and genuine anticipation of what was to come.

It didn't feel like a delay; it felt like destiny. Everything that happened afterward built on the momentum and expectation that our time of waiting generated.

You have been there before—at the ball game or the concert, with absolutely no plan to jump up and wave to strangers you have never met and can barely even see. Yet as the wave moved through the crowd, you found yourself responding to what they started and returning the greeting when it was your moment.

Every time I look to the Scriptures and acknowledge the wave of faith those before me held until they reached the other side, I feel the prompt to wave right back in faith. And suddenly our stories are intertwined, not so distant but connected by the Creator calling us home.

Let this moment we have together now be filled with an awareness of the wave of faith that has swept through history, each man and woman of faith taking their stand at their time, spurring each generation on to the work and wonder of the wait.

God has given you a picture of eternity for you to hold on to in the here and now, just as he did with your brothers and sisters before you.

Where is your heart in the wait?

Wherever you are, know that you are not isolated; you are surrounded by "a great cloud of witnesses" (Hebrews 12:1). Can you hear the testimonies of the overcomers who have made it home, calling over the banisters of heaven to you now?

Moses says, "Answer the Lord today; say, 'Here I am!'" (Exodus 3:4, paraphrase).

David proclaims, "Wait on the LORD; be of good courage, and He shall strengthen your heart; wait, I say, on the LORD!" (Psalm 27:14 NKJV).

Jeremiah declares, "The LORD is good to those who wait for him, to the soul who seeks him" (Lamentations 3:25).

Joshua challenges, "Be strong and courageous" (Joshua 1:9).

Isaiah prophesies, "They who wait for the LORD shall renew their strength; they shall mount up with wings like eagles;

they shall run and not be weary; they shall walk and not faint" (40:31).

Esther's life reminds you, "You were born for such a time as this" (Esther 4:14, paraphrase).

Corrie ten Boom says, "Never be afraid to trust an unknown future to a known God."[7]

Charles Spurgeon preaches, "The Lord's people have always been a waiting people."[8]

And my faith-filled grandpa repeats what he always did on earth: "The best is yet to come!"

Each day your heart can wave at the real eternal home you're headed toward and be filled with wonder in the work of the wait.

As we conclude this conversation together, the deepest prayer of my heart is that you would wave to your inheritance from afar until it is your reality. You are not at the end; this is only the beginning.

So, *will you live in the wait?*

Will you look up and find yourself *eye to eye* with the Savior?

Will you *sow in the dark* and let every tear reap a future harvest?

Bring your daily incense offering to God, your decisive yes, and watch it create a fragrance upon the altar, filling every space you're in and delighting his heart.

Listen for the Father calling to *the warrior within* you, leading you not to fix the facade of your life but to establish eternal strength *deep in your soul instead.* Hear him knocking at the door of your heart and invite him in. Let him *connect the dots* in a way only your Creator could.

Whether you're on a mountaintop or *in the wilderness,* stay close to him—knowing if you *make space* and *lean into the wind,* you will soar! *Live the dream,* right here and now, by saying *yes, and amen* to every promise of God before you see it.

And remember, if he says to wait, you have reason to say, "This must be the place." As you celebrate the wait, the Lord will be your *song for every season*, because *this is a God story*, start to finish.

This is the work and the wonder of the wait. This is the slow burn.

You are walking with a multitude of citizens of heaven who span generations, faithfully singing along the way, "God, you are my strength, my song, and my salvation." All of creation groans and anticipates the day our slow burn will erupt in the explosive fulfillment of every promise. We may groan inwardly, but we also wait eagerly! In the end there will be no doubt that he is the God who redeems and works all things together for good. Just you wait.

The slow burn is burning toward our eternal hope.

Together we wave and say, "Come, Lord Jesus. For you alone our soul waits."

The Waiting Room

On the morning our first son, Wyatt Wesley Wilkerson, was born, we were packed and prepared for our date with destiny. My parents rode in the car with us to the hospital, sitting next to the empty car seat with radiant smiles. My brothers and sister met us in the hospital lobby, and we giddily made our way to the maternity ward. I'd be having a C-section due to a prior injury.

After Rich and I met with the head nurse and registered, she said, "Please take your seat in the waiting room until it's time." So we found the small space where our loved ones as well as many other strangers were sitting.

I chuckled as I slowly eased my swollen body into a plastic chair. While I was surprised we were sitting in the waiting room, not getting comfortable in our own room, I wasn't angry, disappointed, or even impatient. It was the best moment of my life so far. I was simply bemused that once again my expectations didn't line up with reality. This pregnant woman was ready to *go*!

But it was not time to walk. It was time to wait.

I never would have guessed it, but the time in that waiting room turned out to be one of my favorite parts of the day. After eight years of being in the waiting room of life, asking God when I would get to walk out of this season and through a new door,

I had learned to not underestimate the wait. Delays hold destiny. And it felt fitting that I would get one more opportunity to wait that miraculous morning.

Now, I realize that not all waiting rooms hold people anticipating the birth of new life. There have been other waiting rooms I've sat in where I've received heartbreaking news about devastating loss. But the waiting room I am speaking of here is the space of waiting for new purpose to unfold, something we all have experienced in different ways.

Here are a few things I have learned in the waiting room of life.

First, the waiting room is always packed.

If you feel like you are the only one waiting, you probably have your eyes closed and ears covered. As you sift through this season of trusting God, there are others around you in the same place. Some are waiting for purpose and direction; others await relational healing, emotional restoration, or the salvation of a loved one. Building relationships with them will become like gold to you.

Pause to consider this: Could your wait be more than just about yourself? Could your delay be awakening you to others around you in need? Your community and church are full of people waiting.

Boy, was the room packed that morning as I waited for my name to be called. Most people were strangers, of course—but they wouldn't be for long.

Second, the waiting room is great for conversation.

This is where the Louisiana girl in me kicks into high gear. Sure, it's 8:00 a.m. Sure, we're tired. Sure, I've got nerves working overtime as I approach the unknown. *Buuuuut* we all are here in this waiting room together. We might as well get to know each other, right?

You see, conversations turn cold waiting rooms into cozy living rooms where you aren't waiting; you're living. Conversations turn strangers into community. Conversations take your mind off yourself and open your heart to the plight of someone else's journey.

Following my parents' lead, our family started to get to know the other families next to us. We laughed together and took family photos for one another. As the wait extended, we exchanged stories and sang my mom's hit song from my childhood, "Let's Make a Memory While We Wait." We discussed the profound thought that waiting can hold moments you can go on to hold for a lifetime. When you believe that truth, the space to wait takes on a life of its own.

Third, the waiting room is a great place to celebrate others.

My husband knows how to make moments. I am the one in the relationship always concerned that we'll disrupt those around us. He, on the other hand, is the one who cranks up the music and yells, "Let's dance!" And, believe it or not, that is exactly what we did that morning in the waiting room. Our phones became turntables, and the entire family jumped up and started to dance! Who says the waiting room of your life must be dead and boring? The waiting room is what you make it.

If you open your eyes to the people around you and build relationships as you wait, you can celebrate their wins as if they were your own. Instead of being jealous when someone else's name is called to leave the waiting room, you can cheer them on because you know their story. Celebration of others destroys jealousy, just like prayer destroys bitterness.

Before I ever celebrated the birth of my son, I celebrated countless friends as their families grew. That morning in the waiting room, I got to celebrate with several other families first. And when it was my turn, I had a whole room, many of the people I hadn't known hours earlier, celebrating with me.

As I walked out the doors holding Rich's hand, I was thankful for the wait. Finally, I was walking instead of waiting. Could the wait have made the walk even richer?

The wait gave me time to empathize with others, reflect, and pray. To connect and enlarge our circle of support. To realize my story is only a tiny part of the life story God is telling through history. And all our stories are connected.

Eight years of waiting offered me countless opportunities.

Opportunities to isolate or communicate.

Opportunities to doubt or trust.

Opportunities to run away or rest in the finished work of Jesus.

I wouldn't take one day of the journey back. It took me a long time, but I finally came to a place where I realized that, even if I never received a miracle, there is a constant supply of peace and joy just for me right here in this waiting room.

The biggest miracle is that Jesus is enough. You can take him at his word. He *brings life* in the waiting.

So party on in the wait!

Journal Appendix

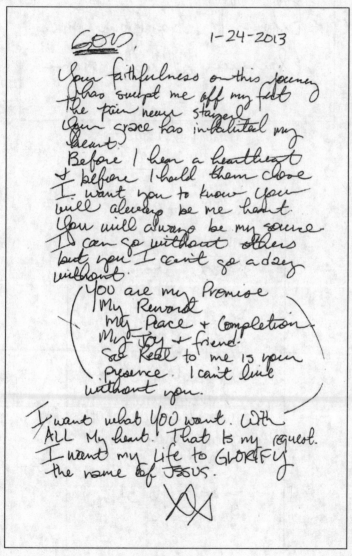

GOD,   1-24-2013

Your faithfulness on this journey
has swept me off my feet
The pain never stayed
Your grace has infiltrated my
heart
Before I hear a heartbeat
& before I hold them close
I want you to know. You
will always be me heart.
You will always be my source
I can go without others
but you I can't go a day
without.

(YOU are my Promise
My Reward
My Peace + Completion
My Joy + friend.
So Real to me is your
presence. I can't live
without you.

I want what YOU want. With
ALL My heart. That is my request.
I want my life to GLORIFY
the name of JESUS.

a) January 24, 2013

233

b) *January 24, 2013*

> Before you life began
> Before It Was Your Time
> You were already mine

> "'They that
> wait on the
> Lord shall
> renew thier
> strength they
> shall mount
> up with wings
> as eagles, They
> shall run &
> not be weary
> walk and not
> faint."
>
> Isaih 40:31
> John 3:16

c) *1993, DawnChere's Bible at 9 years old, referenced on page 16*

Psalm 126:5-6

Those who sow in tears
shall reap with shouts of joy!
He who goes out weeping,
bearing the seed for sowing,
shall come home with shouts
of joy, bringing her sheaves w/her.

SOW IN TEARS

4-28-17

This verse set alight in my heart
this Friday morning. Even in broken
seasons where all we have is our
tears — God says we bear a seed for
sowing. The writer writes of joy
being the emotion as we reap — not
specifically what the harvest actually
is. I'm sure it changes depending upon
the seed of the tears.

Hannah - tears of trust + honesty
David - tears of repentance
woman w/ Alabaster box - adoration

→ all eventually reaped their
harvest with ~~the~~ a heart of joy.

your state in life when you sow
will have changed by the time you
reap. Why? Because what you
have sown has brought a harvest.

Too often we choose not to sow
because of our current state but
we fail to recognize it is
only by sowing that our state
begins to change.

Tears→Seen. Shouts of Joy
—HEARD. The people at home
knew she was coming + bringing a
harvest with her.

I don't know the seed she sowed but I
know it was her faithfulness to the
plot that allowed her to see the
harvest. Too often our tears silence
us. But we must continue to sow.
As you sow - know God—sees you + sees
your tears. Rest assured. As you trust
He will do what only He can do

d) *April 8, 2017, referenced on page 42*

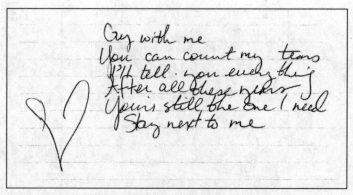

Cry with me
You can count my tears
I'll tell you everything
After all these years
You're still the one I need
Stay next to me

e) *March 2022, referenced on page 50*

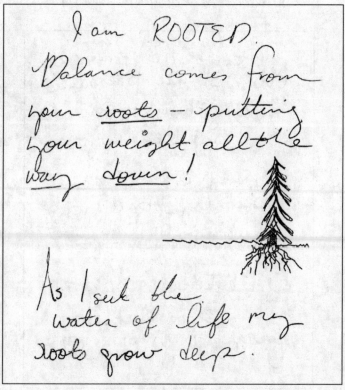

I am ROOTED.
Balance comes from
your _roots_ — putting
your weight all the
way _down!_

As I seek the
water of life my
roots grow deep.

f) *April 5, 2017, referenced on page 76*

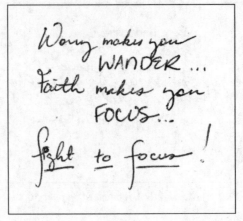

Worry makes you WANDER...
Faith makes you FOCUS...
fight to focus!

g) *November 19, 2017, referenced on page 114*

Jan 17/12 Prayer Call

do not Be pressured
in any thing you
are not Ready for

I have a call on
your life and you
have lots of work to
do
at the time apointed
not in years But like
Sarah I will visit
u

h) *January 17, 2012, referenced on page 122*

MAKE SPACE
FOR GOD.

He wants to fill it.

Where am I making
SPACE.

i) 2016, referenced on page 123

I take deep breaths, kinda like trying to catch my breath on the inside because even the thought of the possibility of it happening is too glorious for words. I pause my expectations to remind myself of where my hope comes from. + feels a bit like cracking the door open into a room filled to the brim w/ gifts, light + wonder and the closing it shut and reminding yourself that you are so happy in the hallway. Because of course the worst thing would be to swing the door wide open run into the room — and allow the wonder and joy to rush over you and flood your emotions + soul + then be asked to LEAVE. Escorted back into the hallway — its not time for this yet. So I protect my heart — I will experience that fullness when it is fully mine.

→

Planning baby showers, choosing room colors & researching brands I am not. I will wait for the day I know my season has arrived and even then I know it will simply be about holding the precious one. I could care less about the shopping, showers & products at this point. The joy will come from Gods promise fulfilled. He will set all my glory.

j) January 2016, referenced on page 134

The Room Is Named the Wonder of Your Grace — & I am NEVER locked out. I am never excorted out. I am never ushered to another hallway.
My Perspective Is My Power.
Dont have time to explore options for my response
God says BREATHE - DEEPLY!
Stop holding your breath — BREATHE ME IN.
Deeply, liberally, aggressively, excessively BREATHE now!

k) January 2016, referenced on page 134

She is NOT AFRAID
of bad news;
her heart is FIRM,
trusting in the LORD.
Her heart is STEADY;
She will NOT be AFRAID.

Ps. 112, 7,8

1) *April 11, 2017, referenced on page 144*

Though you have not seen HIM, you LOVE him. Though you do not now see HIM, you believe in HIM and rejoice with Joy that is inexpressible and filled with glory, obtaining the outcome of your faith, the salvation of your SOULS   1 PETER 1:8-9

May 2, 2017
This verse always romances me. I love the imagery. I love every part of it. It's the TRUTH.
The last few weeks have been hard for me to decipher what is TRUTH. My temper swells, my mind runs, my emotions overflow.

The hard thing for me right now is the highs & lows I feel. But its mostly lows. Restless. angry. I really need the peace of God. I just need to WAIT.

WAIT. WAIT. WAIT. WAIT.

So I speak to my heart.

I Am Strong in You.
Let me Be Still & Know
You are In Control.

m) *May 2, 2017, referenced on page 165*

We discussed ops — Rich
could preach. We began
to pray. I had a hard time
speaking, my tears were flowing.
Then I remembered my sermon
+ felt like I needed the one
— I could barely get it out
but I say, God I look to You
always, I will love you.
Lord my strength. This is
the song I had planned to
close my message with
that night. I talked with
Rich + we both knew we weren't
gonna go to ER w/it not helping
anything. We would wait
till morning to know if our
son was OK.
As we talked in the bathroom
we both were coming to the
conclusion that I should
preach. I'm not gonna stay
home while VJ soldiers.
By now it was 6:30.
I said, I'm gonna do it,
I can + I will + I'm gonna
punch the enemy in the
face. I texted a handful
of leaders to update + ask
for prayer. Got dressed
+ headed to Church
As I pulled up I could sense
the battle. My heart was
focused on the night. The

desperation of my soul.
evaporated every self conscious
or insecure thought. I was
empowered by grace. Focused
by my queen Phil. As desperate
for God's presence as I have
ever been. The team got
me a stool + high top + I
laid down in back during
worship. I walked
to the side of the stage +
made a decision — I am going
to preach like there are two
of us. You are with me
my little man. You are right
here with me. I walked
out on stage to a packed
house of sisters. A real
community. There was an
ease and grace from the
first moment. God had it.
I knew it. I preached w/
everything in me + I preached
to my self. GOD is my
strength, my song + has
become my salvation.
God moved powerfully + I felt
him as strongly as I ever
have in my entire life.
I ended the sermon
low as I spoke on be still
+ know. Bang GOD, I look to
you as their heads were
bowed. Worship washed
across the room. We stood
hands lifted + declared GOD
Halleluyah our GOD reigns

I know God had prepared that
moment.
       In the morning we heard
WILDE WESLEY WILKERSON's
heart beat.   We prayed
God moves at our _weakest._

n) March 15, 2019, referenced on page 168

♡ DAY + NIGHT — DC April 2017

You set the moon a faithful witness in the sky
vs1   Of Comfort In The Night
       You Set the Sun Ablaze Its Glory Testifies
       Of the Greatest light

Pre   I hear you whisper In The midnight hour
      I see your mercy As The Dawn Breaks Out

      DAY and NIGHT
      You SATISFY my Soul
C   DAY and NIGHT
      I'll never WALK ALONE

      You are with me every moment
      You have chosen to be near
B   You are faithful
      You are able
        Your LOVE never fails

o) April 2017, referenced on page 182

Am I
TROSTWORTHY
with the LITTLE?

p) *2016, referenced on page 201*

As surely as I sit
today with pen and paper
within my temporary home,
One day I will stand before
my Father and my Savior
in Heaven. It will be my
reality. Lord let me focus
on the unseen, That which
is the supply of eternity.

PAUSE.

The Day will come

q) *January 2017, referenced on page 220*

Tomorrow is the day. I really feel like I'm pregnant. I don't know, I just have been feeling strange pinches etc in my abdomen. I try not to think about it much. I don't give myself pep talks but somehow I have found an image to meditate on when my mind goes there. I envision a clean white sheet of paper in my journal + writing the positive results of the blood test. 3 words I will save for that moment. "I am _____". I think on it and agree in my heart as I trust God that this is it.

I have peace. The cold sores tell me my body is feeling funny so I'm praying for peace when the systems of my being as well. They will be done. I've been thinking a lot on the 9 months of pregnancy. I think my outlook is that I have been carrying almost 8 yrs. Everyone knows this is 9 mo. but w/me I don't know LOL. I just know I'm carrying ♡

May 17, 2017

I am pregnant

May 19, 2017

Tonight I finish a chapter in my life. Somehow I also finish this journal's last page. It has brought so much comfort to me over the last 5 months. My thought, fears, God's promises, sunday messages and song lyrics have filled the pages + tomorrow I start a new one. But like an old friend I'll return to remember again + again, the heart convos that marked this season + the faithful whisper of heaven. Jesus I ask that the peace you have given us all would reach the hearts of those still waiting. Day + night, satisfy their souls like only you can. Let their cup overflow even in the wait with your steadfast love.

Selah.

May 19, 2017

Acknowledgments

Rich: This book wouldn't be written if it weren't for you. Your encouragement, partnership, creativity, and celebration through every part of this journey are only a microcosm of what you do in every area of our life. You amaze me.

Wyatt, Wilde, Waylon, and Wolfgang: Our relationship has revealed God's love to me in ways I could never have dreamed. So glad you are on this earth. Jesus in you is what our world needs. Trust him. You are cherished.

Mom and Dad: My heroes. I reference you more than any historian or famous thinker. You are that and so much more to me. May I show up for my children the way you have for us since day one. My sisters and brothers: Destiny, Phil, Denny, Sarah, Dez, Lucas, Bri, Dee, Pilar, Dakota, and Blaire: I love writing your names and I delight in your company and camaraderie. Thanks for loving me. Grammy: You are the OG. A marvel. We adore you.

VOUS Church: No place I'd rather be. Love you dearly. Let's play the long game. Miami: You changed my life, and your best days are ahead.

Gabby: Your feedback, friendship, and faith on this journey has blessed me. Pamela: Thank you for your wisdom, grace, and listening ear. Carrie: From the first letter I received from you, something was so different. I have treasured this adventure.

You are incredible. Thank you. The entire team at W: Your unity, enthusiasm, and excellence are inspiring. It's an honor to be a part.

Truthfully, I could write a book of all the people who have loved and built me along this road of life. Since I was a little girl, I have been extravagantly loved and I don't want to overlook one act of kindness. For every seed sown in my soul of faith, generosity, and love, thank you.

There are countless people around the world who prayed for us on one side of our miracle as we waited and then celebrated on the other. I may not get to thank you face-to-face until heaven but know that one day I will.

Notes

Chapter 1

1. Ronald Rolheiser, *The Holy Longing: The Search for a Christian Spirituality* (Random House, 1999), 103.
2. Mark H. McCormack, *What They Don't Teach You at Harvard Business School* (Bantam Books, 1984), 169.
3. Charles R. Swindoll, *Abraham: One Nomad's Amazing Journey of Faith* (Tyndale, 2014), 8.
4. Latin Is Simple, "incendere," accessed November 11, 2024, https://www.latin-is-simple.com/en/vocabulary/verb/189.
5. "Humans Can Distinguish at Least One Trillion Different Odors," HHMI, March 20, 2014, https://www.hhmi.org/news/humans-can-distinguish-least-one-trillion-different-odors.
6. "The Waiting," by Tom Petty, produced by Tom Petty and Jimmy Iovine, *Hard Promises*, Backstreet Records, 1981.
7. Charles Spurgeon, *The Treasury of David: The Complete Seven Volumes*, vol. VII (Bible Study Steps, 2016), Kindle.
8. Despina Stavrinos et al., "Impact of Distracted Driving on Safety and Traffic Flow," *Accident Analysis & Prevention* 61 (2013): 63–70, https://doi.org/10.1016/j.aap.2013.02.003.

Chapter 2

1. "Benefits of Sauna Bathing for Heart Health," UCLA Health, February 1, 2023, https://www.uclahealth.org/news/article/benefits-sauna-bathing-heart-health.

2. John Ortberg, *If You Want to Walk on Water, You've Got to Get Out of the Boat* (Zondervan, 2001), 217.

CHAPTER 3

1. Luke 10:38–42; John 1:47–50; Luke 5:22.
2. Mark 7:31–37; Matthew 9:36; Matthew 19:16–22.
3. Matthew 9:20–22.
4. Mark 1:17.
5. John 4:7–15.
6. Matthew 14.
7. Mark 5:3–20.
8. 1 Corinthians 2:9
9. A. W. Tozer, *The Pursuit of God* (BroadStreet Publishing, 2007), 59.
10. Purrven Bajjaj, "Development of the Eye," accessed November 10, 2024, https://plano.co/eye-conditions/development-of-the-eye/.
11. Bajjaj, "Development of the Eye."

CHAPTER 4

1. I've had this definition on my wall my whole life from a name company.
2. St. John of the Cross, "Dark Night of the Soul," from *The Dark Night of the Soul*, trans. David Lewis (Thomas Baker, 1908), https://www.poetryfoundation.org/poems/157984/the-dark-night-of-the-soul; Saint Teresa of Avila, *The Interior Castle*, or *Las Moradas (The Mansions)* (1588).
3. T. S. Eliot, *Murder in the Cathedral* (Harcourt Brace & Co., 1935), 86.
4. Vaishali Singh, "Discover the Art of Forcing Rhubarb," *Small Farm Canada*, accessed November 10, 2024, https://www.smallfarmcanada.ca/gardens-crops/discover-the-art-of-forcing-rhubarb/; Eric Grundhauser, "Listen to the Sick Beats of Rhubarb Growing in the Dark," Atlas Obscura, April 10, 2018, https://www.atlasobscura.com/articles/forced-rhubarb-makes-sound.
5. Bede, *The History of the English Church and People* (Barnes & Noble Books, 2005), XXVII.
6. C. S. Lewis, *Till We Have Faces: A Myth Retold* (HarperOne, 2017), 58.
7. "Let It Flow," lyrics by Rich Wilkerson, VOUS Worship, 2024.

8. "Wildflowers," National Park Service, July 2024, https://www.nps
.gov/deva/learn/nature/wildflowers.htm.

9. Augustine, *Confessions*, trans. Henry Chadwick (Oxford University
Press, 2009), 50.

10. Timothy Keller, *Walking with God Through Pain and Suffering*
(Penguin Publishing Group, 2015), 304.

CHAPTER 5

1. Eugene Peterson, *The Pastor: A Memoir* (HarperOne, 2012), 8.

2. Nelson Mandela, *Long Walk to Freedom: The Autobiography of Nelson
Mandela* (Little, Brown and Company, 1995), 622.

3. Rick Warren, *The Purpose Driven Life: What on Earth Am I Here For?*
(Zondervan, 2002), 18.

4. John 6:35, 8:12, 10:9, 11, 11:17, 14:6, 15:1.

CHAPTER 6

1. Encyclopedia.com, "establish," accessed November 11, 2024, https://
www.encyclopedia.com/social-sciences-and-law/law/law/establish.

2. "Hurricane Andrew: 30 Year Anniversary," National Weather
Service, accessed December 29, 2024, https://www.weather.gov
/lmk/HurricaneAndrew30Years.

3. Paola Rosa-Aquino, "Palm Trees Bend in High Winds and Are Hard
to Uproot. A Forest Ecologist Says They're Perfectly Designed to
Withstand Hurricanes," Business Insider, October 4, 2022, https://
www.businessinsider.com/palm-trees-adapted-to-withstand
-hurricanes-forest-ecologist-says-2022-10.

4. Ecclesiastes 4:12.

5. Anne Graham Lotz, quoted in "Why Did Lazarus Have to Die?"
BeliefNet, April 2004, https://www.beliefnet.com/faiths/christianity
/2004/04/why-did-lazarus-have-to-die.aspx.

6. James 1:7–8.

7. "Why Women Live Longer in Okinawa, Japan," *Modern Age* (blog),
November 7, 2023, https://www.modern-age.com/blog/why-women
-live-longer-in-okinawa-japan.

8. Dallas Willard, *The Divine Conspiracy* (HarperCollins, 1998), 11.

9. Willard, *The Divine Conspiracy*, 72.

CHAPTER 7

1. C. S. Lewis, *Mere Christianity* (HarperCollins, 2001), 49.
2. *Fast Food Market Size, Industry Share & COVID-19 Impact Analysis, by Product Type (Burger & Sandwich, Pizza & Pasta, Asian & Latin American Food, and Others), Service Type (On-Premise and Delivery & Take Away), and Regional Forecast, 2021–2028*, report, Fortune Business Insights, last updated December 16, 2024, https://www .fortunebusinessinsights.com/fast-food-market-106482#.
3. Psalm 23:5.

CHAPTER 8

1. Desmond Tutu, *The Words of Desmond Tutu*, ed. Naomi Tutu (Newmarket Press, 1989), 71.
2. Mark Atteberry, *The Samson Syndrome: What You Can Learn from the Baddest Boy in the Bible* (Thomas Nelson, 2014), 97.
3. Tim Keller, *The Reason for God: Belief in an Age of Skepticism* (Penguin Random House, 2008), 223–24.
4. Sergey Edunov et al., "Three and a Half Degrees of Separation," Meta (blog), February 4, 2016, https://research.facebook.com/blog /2016/2/three-and-a-half-degrees-of-separation/.
5. "Stellar Life Cycle," Earth Science, accessed December 4, 2024, https://courses.lumenlearning.com/suny-earthscience/chapter /stellar-life-cycle/.
6. "The Nearest Neighbor Star," Imagine the Universe!, NASA, updated December 8, 2020, https://imagine.gsfc.nasa.gov/features /cosmic/nearest_star_info.html.
7. C. S. Lewis, *The Voyage of the Dawn Treader* (Geoffrey Bles, 1952), 209.

CHAPTER 9

1. John 8:1–11, Matthew 8:1–3, Mark 5:1–20, Mark 2:1–12, Matthew 26:7, Luke 23:40–43.
2. "Stuck in a Moment You Can't Get Out Of," by Bono and The Edge, on U2, *All That You Can't Leave Behind*, produced by Daniel Lanois and Brian Eno, Island/Interscope Records, 2000.
3. Henri Nouwen, *Turn My Mourning into Dancing: Finding Hope During Hard Times* (W Publishing, 2001), 13.

4. Ellen Vaughn, *Becoming Elisabeth Elliot* (B&H Publishing Group, 2020), 11.

5. Matthias R. Mehl et al., "Are Women Really More Talkative Than Men?," *Science* 317, no. 5834 (2007): 82, https://doi.org/10.1126 /science.1139940.

6. Lydia Smith, "Scientists 'Bust the Myth' That Venting Helps Reduce Anger," *Newsweek*, March 20, 2024, https://www.newsweek.com /scientists-bust-myth-venting-anger-1881252.

7. Luke 6:45.

8. Proverbs 18:21.

9. Matthew 6:26–28.

10. "Swamp of Sadness," *The NeverEnding Story*, directed by Wolfgang Petersen, produced by Bavaria Film, distributed by Warner Bros, 1984.

11. Chris Woodyard, "Top 16 Longest Gaps Between Interstate Exits," *USA Today*, August 13, 2011, https://content.usatoday.com /communities/driveon/post/2011/08/longest-distances-between -exits-on-US-freeways-415029/1#.UDl9OKPy2So.

12. Samuel Henderson, *Baader-Meinhof Phenomenon: Why Do We Keep Noticing Certain Things More Often?* (pub. by author, 2023), https://a .co/d/30YtKtp.

Chapter 10

1. Walter Farley, *The Black Stallion* (Random House, 1941).

2. 1 Samuel 17.

3. "It's Time for You to Lay Aside Every Unnecessary Weight," Renner Ministries, May 30, 2024, https://renner.org/article/its-time-for -you-to-lay-aside-every-unnecessary-weight/.

4. A. W. Tozer, *The Pursuit of God* (BroadStreet, 2007), 28.

Chapter 11

1. Steve Younis, "When Did Superman First Fly?" Superman Homepage, September 22, 2022, https://www.supermanhomepage.com/when -did-superman-first-fly/.

2. Numbers 13:30 NIV.

3. Acts 2:41.

CHAPTER 12

1. Amy Irvine, "Hiroo Onoda: The Japanese Soldier Who Refused to Surrender," History Hit, September 28, 2023, https://www.historyhit.com/hiroo-onoda-the-japanese-soldier-who-refused-to-surrender/.
2. *Oxford English Dictionary*, "celebrate," accessed December 30, 2024, https://www.oed.com/dictionary/celebrate_v?tl=true.
3. Acts 16.
4. Dietrich Bonhoeffer, *God Is in the Manger: Reflections on Advent and Christmas* (Presbyterian Publishing Corporation, 2012).
5. Dietrich Bonhoeffer to Karl and Paula Bonhoeffer, letter, November 29, 1943, Tegel Prison, "Advent: Week One," in Bonhoeffer, *God Is in the Manger*, 3.
6. "Let's Make a Memory While We Wait," by DeAnza Duron, Little Destiny Publishing, Inc., 1984.
7. Melissa Russell, "Why Celebrating Small Wins Matters," *Harvard Summer School* (blog), May 30, 2024, https://summer.harvard.edu/blog/why-celebrating-small-wins-matters/.
8. Mark Travers, "A Psychologist Explains the Neuroscience of Your 'Gratitude Practice,'" *Forbes*, June 4, 2024, https://www.forbes.com/sites/traversmark/2024/05/22/a-psychologist-explains-how-to-hack-your-brains-gratitude-circuit/.
9. Teresa M. Amabile and Steven J. Kramer, "The Power of Small Wins," *Harvard Business Review*, May 2011, https://hbr.org/2011/05/the-power-of-small-wins.
10. Madhuleena Roy Chowdhury, "The Neuroscience of Gratitude and Effects on the Brain," Positive Psychology, April 9, 2019, https://positivepsychology.com/neuroscience-of-gratitude/.

CHAPTER 13

1. Corrie ten Boom, *Tramp for the Lord*, ed. Jamie Buckingham (CLC Publications, 2011), 125.
2. "Won't You Be My Neighbor," by Fred M. Rogers, McFeely-Rogers Foundation, 1990, https://www.misterrogers.org/video-playlist/mister-rogers-songs/.
3. "Baby Shark Dance," Pinkfong, June 17, 2016, YouTube, 2:16, https://www.youtube.com/watch?v=XqZsoesa55w.

4. Gottfried Schlaug et al., "From Singing to Speaking: Facilitating Recovery from Nonfluent Aphasia," *Future Neurology* 5, no. 5 (September 21, 2010): 657–65, doi:10.2217/fnl.10.44.

5. "Teddy Mac—The Songaminute Man," The Songaminute Man, website accessed November 13, 2024, https://songaminuteman.com/.

6. M. Castillo, "Listening to Music," *American Journal of Neuroradiology* 31, no. 9 (2010): 1549–50, https://doi.org/10.3174/ajnr.A2076.

7. "Promoting Social-Emotional Development Through Music: Practical Activities," Everyday Speech, August 18, 2023, https://everydayspeech.com/sel-implementation/promoting-social-emotional-development-through-music-practical-activities/.

8. Psalm 19:14, 40:2, 23:4.

9. "We Shall Overcome," published as "We Will Overcome," in *The People's Songs Bulletin*, 1947.

10. "God I Look to You," by Jenn Johnson and Ian McIntosh, Bethel Music Publishing (ASCAP), 2010.

11. "God I Look to You," Johnson and McIntosh.

CHAPTER 14

1. Robert Kleck and Angelo Strenta, "Perceptions of the Impact of Negatively Valued Physical Characteristics on Social Interaction," *Journal of Personality and Social Psychology* 39, no. 5 (1980): 861–73, https://doi.org/10.1037/0022-3514.39.5.861.

2. John 20:24–27.

CHAPTER 15

1. Joshua Liebman, *Peace of Mind* (Simon & Schuster, 1946).

2. Barry Schwartz, *The Paradox of Choice: Why More Is Less*, rev. ed. (HarperCollins, 2009), chapter 11.

3. Dietrich Bonhoeffer, *Life Together: The Classic Exploration of Christian Community* (HarperOne, 2009), 27.

4. Martin Luther King Jr., "I Have a Dream," speech, Lincoln Memorial, Washington, DC, August 28, 1963.

CHAPTER 16

1. "Jodi Benson Recording Part of Your World (Long Version)," Pillsbury

Giggles, January 14, 2019, YouTube, 6:31, https://www.youtube.com /watch?v=AWTJkyLWgrk.

2. Romans 8:26.

CHAPTER 17

1. "Tears in Heaven," by Eric Clapton and Will Jennings, *Rush: Music from the Motion Picture Soundtrack*, published by Warner/Chappell Music, Inc., Universal Music Publishing Group, 1991.

2. "It's Just About Time for Me to Lay Down My Cross," by The Hinsons, track 1 on *We Promise You Gospel*, Calvary Records, 1973.

3. N. T. Wright, *Surprised by Hope: Rethinking Heaven, the Resurrection, and the Mission of the Church* (HarperCollins, 2008), 41.

4. Caroline Leaf, *Think and Eat Yourself Smart: A Neuroscientific Approach to a Sharper Mind and Healthier Life* (Baker Publishing Group, 2016), 142.

5. C. S. Lewis, *Mere Christianity* (Geoffrey Bles, 1952), 134.

6. John Suchet, *Beethoven: The Man Revealed* (Atlantic Monthly Press, 2013).

7. Corrie ten Boom, *Clippings from My Notebook* (Thomas Nelson, 1982), 27.

8. Charles Spurgeon, *The Treasury of David* (Bible Study Steps, 2016).

About the Author

DawnCheré Wilkerson is a speaker, singer, songwriter, and local pastor who loves nothing more than to encourage people of all ages to never give up. After an eight-year journey through infertility, DawnCheré and her husband, Rich, have seen the faithfulness of God as they have welcomed their four children, Wyatt, Wilde, Waylon, and Wolfgang into the world. DawnCheré and Rich are the lead pastors of VOUS Church in Miami, Florida.